PROMISE THEORY

CASE STUDY ON THE 2016 BREXIT VOTE

Jan A. Bergstra and Mark Burgess

Contents

Preface

Brexit offers a rare opportunity to examine a complicated network of intentions and processes, through the lens of promise theory. We examine the arguments and positions surrounding the Brexit process, from the beginning. We argue that promises have played a central role in its unfolding, and that the simple formalities of promise theory are quite helpful in assessing the kinds of claims made, and their likelihood of being realized. The role of trust along side promises is particularly interesting. Perhaps unsurprisingly, one might conclude that, when voters don't know who to trust, their choices are based more on emotional resonance (confirmation bias) than rational assessment. We build a partial inventory of the promises made, and try to assess their role in the discussion.

1

Introduction

Brexit is going to happen, just as global warming and rising sea-levels are going to happen. The choice for the UK to be outside the EU, rather than inside the EU, has been made in an orderly manner, notwithstanding the fact that the way it came about may be criticised from various perspectives. For the purpose of our analysis, Brexit, viewed as an intention (as well as viewed as an action) may be taken as morally neutral, or at least not outright morally wrong. Regardless of the extent to which Brexit is advantageous or damaging for the UK or EU, we elect to disregard the ethical dimension, in order to make an impartial analysis of the process.

Moreover, given the fact that Brexit is going to happen, in one way or another, it is reasonable for all parties involved to try to make the best out of it, whatever that means. Promise theory may well be able to shed some light on this. Given the obvious promise that the UK government intends to turn Brexit into a success, it matters to both UK and EU citizens how each party conceptualises or defines 'success'. Much of the uncertainty lies in the many dependencies and conditionals that are implicit in the promises given, and what they could mean for from an 'EU27' point of view (EU27 is what remains of EU after the UK has left).

The literature on Brexit is already extensive and diverse, so providing a survey of that literature is not feasible in this paper. Oliver 2013 [17] made a detailed survey of the scenario in which the UK might leave the EU (not yet using the term Brexit), sketched out how it might come about, and the ramifications if might have. By now some of the scenarios discussed by Oliver have been ruled out by recent events while some of the predictions made in [17] seem to have been quite accurate.

The arguments for and against Brexit exist in various level of abstraction, ranging from imprecise slogans to detailed legal and economic arguments about problematic aspects concerning the design and functioning of the EU. Minford et.al. 2015 [15] provide a systematic account of pro Leave arguments. This account highlights why it is so difficult to find unambiguous arguments for either position. For example, it has been posited that Brexit would be bad for UK science and technology, because these activities profit so much from the EU framework. Minford et. al., however, are unimpressed by this objection, because they perceive the EU as a sophisticated protectionist organisation which supports and maintains only its allies, in the member states, by way of subsidies and clientism; the science community being a visible example of that phenomenon. Many other examples exist, with varying biases.

1.1 Promise theory as a novel perspective on Brexit

Promise theory as a practical tool for systems design and analysis has been put forward by Mark Burgess and co-authors in a sequence of papers. A recent summary of promise theory is Bergstra & Burgess 2014 [1], for a popular introduction see Burgess 2015 [3].[1] Thinking in terms of promises is both intuitively appealing and flexible in terms of meaning. Promise theory is not based on a philosophical analysis of the concept of a promise. Rather it takes a liberal conception of promises as a point of departure for an engineering style analysis. This liberal viewpoint is taken to the extreme by insisting that promises, as used within promise theory, do not necessarily create obligations. The penalty, if any, of not keeping a promise by its promiser lies entirely in the degradation of trust it enjoys from other agents, which the promiser may incur as a consequence. A few other basic results are pertinent. In particular an agent (any party) is responsible for only its own promises and actions, and no agent may make a promise on behalf of another agent with any certainty[2]. We shall see this criterion violated again and again in what follows.

Promise theory takes for granted that animate as well as inanimate agents can produce promises, and that systems evolve in part by creating and processing

---

[1] Promise theory may be considered more formal and extended rendering of ANT (see Latour 2005 [12]).

[2] Promises about one's own actions are called promises of the first kind, and are fundamental. All other promises on behalf of others (second, third, and fourth kinds) are derivative, and are measurably less certain.

bundles of promises. In this paper we will assume that promises are made by human agents, or groups of human agents (see figure 3.2), while insisting that our promises do not automatically imply obligations, either legally or morally.

We plan to examine Brexit from the point of view of this Promise Theory. By considering Brexit from this specific angle, a novel classification of the positions and arguments may emerge to provide some clarity within the noise, and perhaps even additional insight. At the same time, Brexit serves as a very particular kind of case study for the application and further development of promise theory.

Oliver 2017 [19] suggests a classification of theoretical approaches to Brexit in four categories as well as a fifth group of other theories. An approach to Brexit based on promise theory fits in his category 'constructivism and Brexit' as well as in 'other theories'.

1.2 Brexit meets promises

Several aspects of Brexit relate to promises. We don't claim to be comprehensive on that matter, however.

1. In Chapter 2 we discuss the status of the 2016 referendum on EU membership, has it been advisory or binding. This issue is primarily connected with promises made in the Conservative manifesto for the 2015 general election, and in the subsequent Queen's Speech.

2. Several promises (so-called pro Leave promises) about the virtues of Brexit have dominated the final phase of the campaign for the referendum. We will survey these pro-Leave promises in Section 1.5.1.

3. During the campaign for the referendum promises with a pro Remain bias were issued as well, a survey of four core pro Leave promises is given in Section 4.1.

4. Many other arguments for Brexit can be put forward than those which obtained most attention during the campaign for the referendum. Just as the core arguments these secondary arguments can be faithfully rendered as promises. A list of such arguments phrased as promises is provided in Section 4.2.

5. Finding support from the House of Lords by the UK Government for triggering article 50 on the basis of the referendum outcome can be under-

stood as an application of the Salisbury Doctrine, based on the promise concerning the referendum in the 2015 Conservative Manifesto.

6. Apart from the tactical expectation that the Conservative majority in the House of Commons would grow, upon having a general election in June 2017, the 'logical' need for having a general election based on manifestos, which are more specific concerning the choice of appropriate way to move forward to Brexit, is quite obvious. This aspect is discussed in detail in Chapter 7.

7. Brexit provides new and useful opportunities for the remaining part of the EU as well. Such opportunities, some of which may compete with rather than coincide with perceived UK interests, are phrased in terms of promises in Section 6.4.

8. Brexit may potentially constitute a step forward for both the UK and for the remaining EU. This aspect seems to be entirely ignored in the present debate. Such potential advantages are phrased as promises in Section 6.5.

9. The famous assertion 'Brexit is Brexit' may be understood as the promise made by the UK Government that the UK will indeed leave the EU. This promise is given in structured notation in Section 4.3.1 and in the light of its crucial importance it is commented in various other parts of the text.[3]

10. Specific ways of performing Brexit give rise to specific promises about the future link between the UK and various EU institutions or EU related (e.g. EEA, EFTA, the customs union, EURATOM, CJEU, ECHR). Such promises are discussed throughout the text. The most prominent of these promises is Theresa May's famous promise "better no deal than a bad deal", the latter promise is discussed in Section 4.3.1.

1.3 Promises, stated preferences, stated subjective probabilities, and stated opinions

Our emphasis is solely on promises, understood to mean documented intentions in promise theory, though promises occur among a variety of different

---

[3] We notice that it is a mistake to view 'Brexit is Brexit' as a meaningless tautology which it seems to be at first sight. In the logical tradition the alternative for 'Brexit is Brexit' is the non-existence of Brexit. Thus 'Brexit is Brexit' is a non-trivial and thereby meaningful existence statement.

utterances, each of which play an important role in the Brexit process. We distinguish three other forms of expression: stated preferences, stated expectations (with stated differential expectations as a special case), and stated opinions.

1.3.1 Stated preferences

Stating a preference does not commit a person P, stating the preference, to any action. However a person Q, in scope of the statement, may be inclined to lend it weight and form expectations about P's expected behavior upon hearing the statement. Here are some examples of stated preferences from the Brexit debate:

- It is preferable if, in the future, the UK is not bound to the decisions of the ECJU.

- It is preferable if the short term (say until 2015) economic price which the population UK has to pay for Brexit is minimized.

- It is preferable if the UK remains a member of the EU.

- It is preferable if the UK can negotiate bilateral trade agreements all over the world, independently from the EU.

- It is better for voters not to pay much attention to so-called experts when making up their mind in advance of the referendum.

- It is better for the UK to maintain membership of the single market and of the customs union than to leave these as well.

- It is preferable that the referendum outcome is materialized over it not being materialized.

Preferences differ from promises in that there is no notion of keeping a preference. However, making a U-turn on a stated preference by stating an opposite preference, may lead to a reassessment of trust, by agents watching the U-turn.

1.3.2 Stated subjective probabilities

Persons, committees, and organisations may issue statements concerning their assessment of the subjective likelihood of certain events. In the context of Brexit, such statements occur very frequently, though without quantification of

the subjective probabilities at hand. Many statements assert that an assessment
of subjective probability has been changed on the basis of new events. Here are
some examples, paraphrased.

- 'It is very likely that crashing out (in 2019) with a so-called hard Brexit
  will leave the UK in a position where the GDP is lower than would be
  expected otherwise for the first 10 years after 2019.'

- 'In the months following the referendum, no deterioration of the economy
  of the UK was observed. It was stated that it was unlikely that Brexit
  would adversely affect the UK economy.'

- 'One year after the referendum several several economic parameters have
  developed in a negative manner: relatively high inflation, low relative
  growth of the economy in comparison with other EU states, a stall in the
  market for high end houses in London, trade deficit constant rather than
  decreasing in spite of the devaluation of the pound w.r.t. Dollar and Euro.
  Consequently, some observers state that it is likely that Brexit will have
  an adverse impact on the economy.'

- 'After the 2017 general election, some commentators stated that the occurrence of a hard Brexit had become less likely. It has also been stated
  that the occurrence of a so-called transition period has become more
  likely (though the confusion on what may be expected at the end of that
  period persists).'

- 'After two months of seemingly unproductive Brexit negotiations it is said
  that it is less likely that a trade agreement will be agreed upon.'

- 'It is hugely preferable that Labour won't be allowed to take control of
  the government.'

- 'After leaving the EU the UK will be able to obtain a portfolio of useful
  trade agreements with non-EU countries and blocks the impact of which
  will compensate for the increased difficulties regarding trade with EU
  member states.'

Much journalistic coverage on Brexit consists of the stated subjective probabilities of journalists, as well as with reporting about the stated subjective probabilities of other agents. Promises and stated subjective probabilities are closely
related. In Section 1.6 below we will provide a classification of promises including a class of promises labeled as documented expectations. A difference

between stated subjective probabilities and promises (i.e. documented expectations) is that documented expectations are not stated in probabilistic terms. It is up to the promisee to make his or her own subjective assessment of probability for the promise being kept. In the majority of cases subjective probabilities are informally quantified on an ordinal scale using phrases as: unlikely, possible, likely, very likely, almost certain, more likely than before, and less likely than before.

1.3.3 Stated opinions

In promise theory every statement of fact or 'alternative fact'[4] can be understood as a promise. In many cases, however, there is no immediate or direct feedback loop expected between a promise being kept and the trust in the promiser. Many comments about Brexit and the way it unfolds are best labelled simply as opinions. We prefer, in our description of Brexit, to make a distinction between promises and opinions. This is not a feature of promise theory per se. Promise theory is a methodology for systems design; its application, in our perception, need not take into account a disparate or representative collection of opinions. Promise theory has been designed to allow animate as well as inanimate agents take on the role of promisers and promisees, to view intentions directly and by proxy side by side. In the case of Brexit, where all promisers and promisees are animate human beings, this technical aspect of promise theory creates some consternation with lay-readers which we hope to resolve by labelling some as statements opinions. A clear example of this is the assertion used by the chancellor Philip Hammond, that the people have not voted to get poorer. It is somehow unconvincing to label this assertion a promise.

There may also be no intended relation between the promise and the behaviour of the promiser. In such cases we will speak of a stated opinion, and an opinion may range from fact to 'alternative fact'. Many opinions have been stated by different persons involved in the Brexit process.

- The UK pays £350.000.000 per month to the EU.

- The UK pays £250.000.000 per month to the EU.

- Immigration in the UK has spiralled out of control since 2000.

---

[4] The expression 'alternative fact' was coined by US presidential candidate Donald Trump during his election campaign, to discredit unfavourable news coverage that he wanted to discredit as falsely reported.

- Until mid 2017 the UK has never made a realistic attempt to reduce the number of immigrants from other EU members states.

- Since oil prices have dropped in the wake of the financial crisis, Scotland needs external money. Scotland profits so much from support from the UK (read England) that it cannot afford to move towards independence within the UK.

- UK Science and Research profit a lot from EU funding.

- EU regulations contribute positively to food safety in the UK.

- After the Brexit vote far fewer EU citizens from outside the EU are planing to work, or to study, in the UK health sector.

- There is no well-defined notion of a single market in relation to the EU, there are merely different forms of association to the EU, some of which (e.g. Norway) are commonly viewed as being incorporated in an EU single market, though not for all classes of goods and services.

- The referendum outcome that the UK should leave the EU was caused by a Brexiter (Vote Leave) campaign that made use of deceptive promises and lies.

- The referendum outcome was to be expected, irrespective of the campaign of both sides, and irrespective of government support for Remain on the basis of the observation that each previous referendum asking for popular support for the EU or for strengthening the EU had a negative outcome as well. We mention: Norway in 1994 about EU membership, Sweden in 2003 about adopting the Euro, France in 2005 and The Netherlands also in 2005 both about the EU constitution, Greece in 2015 about the joint proposal made by the EU, the ECB, and the IMF, for solving the financial crisis in Greece, and The Netherlands in 2016 about closer ties between Ukraine and the EU.[5]

---

[5] One way to look at this remarkable state of affairs (including the UK referendum, 7 referendums about the EU each with a negative result) is to ascertain a democratic deficit for the EU, another interpretation might be that in many European countries a dangerous form of grass roots nationalism is still very strong in terms of its popular support, and that pro EU politicians are engaged in an ongoing uphill struggle to achieve a degree of unification between European countries that is able to eliminate the risk that oppositions between nations will

- The voters did not vote to get poorer.

- The voters knew very well that life outside the EU would be less prosperous, at least initially, but they deliberately took that risk in view of expected long term strategic advantages.

1.4 Promises, biases, and structured notation

Consider the assertion P = 'Brexit will be a success'. This assertion cannot plausibly be understood as a logical proposition, i.e. one that is either true or false. It could be understood as a kind of prediction, but then there is still no way to say anything about the validity of the prediction. A simpler way to look at P is as a promise made by a promiser A to a promisee B. Rather than assigning a speculative truth value to P, at the time the promise is made, B may keep the promise in mind and may update its assessment of trust in P, in accordance with B's assessment of the validity of P at any moment that suits B. The original belief in the promised outcome (that B assesses upon being promised P by A) depends mainly on the credibility of A in the eyes of B. In a structured notation the promise at hand is rendered as follows[6]:

Promiser. A

Bias. Pro Leave.

Type. [+]

Body. Brexit will be a success for the UK.

Promisee. B.

Assessment. Pending.

Here the indication of the type '[+]' indicates that the promise is about a state of affairs which the promiser claims (promises) will be satisfied at some time, though without any claim that the promiser brings that state of affairs about

---

grow out of hand once more. The Ukrainian crisis demonstrates that without such unification the risk of a military conflict within Europe is still present. Unfortunately working too fast towards European unification can generate stress as well, so that striking an adequate balance is crucial, though difficult.

[6] Note that our notation here differs from that in reference [1]. We use a structured notation rather than a symbolic notation to better accommodate the various aspects of promises that apply to the current case.

by its own action. If the promiser expects to be the causal influence in bring-
ing about the promised outcome, then the type would be denoted + rather than
[+]. More types of promises, marked with −, [−],−!, and [−!] are specified in
Paragraph 1.6 below.

Assessments are made individually by any agent in promise theory. For the
purpose of this paper, we assume that all assessments are made by a hypothetical external observer. Assessments are also made in particular contexts, and
based on what agents believe individually. The expectation that Brexit will be
a success can be formulated by someone who opposes Brexit, i.e. who favours
Remain, or vice versa. For instance a person who initially is pro Leave may
consider the consequences of Leave for the remaining EU to be so adverse that
they oppose Brexit for that reason. When promises are issued, in connection
with a choice that lies ahead, the agent's *bias* may be defined as an assessment
of which outcome the promiser intends the promise to contribute towards. A
bias may also be neutral.

1.5 The central role of promises in the unfolding of Brexit

The referendum of June 23 2016 defined a collective preference for the UK to
leave the EU. At face value one would think that, to comply with the outcome
of the referendum, it would suffice that the UK leaves the EU. However, this
path the opens into a plethora of possible alternatives for future treaties and
protocols for interacting between the different categories of nation. In promise
language, the set of promises implicit in membership must be replaced by a
new set of explicit promises to different collective agents in and around the EU.
The UK might proceed as a member of EEA (this includes, Norway, Iceland,
and Luxembourg along side the EU nations); this is often termed the 'Norway
option'. It is simple in the sense that there is a well defined (and tested) set
of promises associated with an agreement of this type. In Djurkovic & Menon
2016 [6] a survey of 5 options for forthcoming trade relations between UK and
EU27 is given wherein membership of EEA is indicated as being most close to
EU membership.

This relatively clear implementation of Brexit might be considered a transition to non-EU member status with minimal overall impact. However, leading
Brexit proponents and the UK government have both expressed doubts regarding this future, because they claim that 'the Norway option' would compromise
a number of promises that were made by proponents of the UK leaving the EU,
in advance of the referendum. Let us examine these promises.

1.5.1 Four pro Leave promises

1. 'If the UK leaves the EU it will be in full control of all forms of immigration'. However, all EEA members promise to facilitate the free flow of workers to and from the EU.

2. 'Once the UK leaves the EU then subsequently there will be no substantial annual financial transfers from the UK to the EU'. One might exempt transfers that constitute contributions made for participation in very specific EU programs such as the famous Erasmus Program. Moreover, 'the UK will be free to direct these transfer streams to different targets' (for instance the NHS).

3. 'Once the EU leaves the EU, the UK will be free to engage in trade agreements with other states and blocks worldwide.' However, the freedom of trade policy is constrained for EEA members.

4. 'The UK can freely choose which EU regulations to follow', again this is not so for EEA members.

The insistence that these promises be kept is grounded as follows:

- These promises played a very prominent role in final stage of public debate regarding the referendum.

- The people are entitled to see these promises kept, when 'the will of the people to leave the EU' is put into effect. If that does not happen, they will feel betrayed (a breach of trust) with serious consequences for the UK democratic system. This is an inference of a promise about the people's feeling, assumed on their behalf.

- It ought to be justifiable for the UK government to insist that it maintains a high level of trust by the people, and thus has an obligation to draw certain lines. Even opponents of Brexit agree that compliance with promises, made in connection with Brexit, ought to be kept in order to maintain public trust in the UK political system.

Thinking in terms of promises, and viewing the keeping of those promises as buoying levels of trust, is key to these considerations. The alternative interpretation of promises (in law) is that promises impose a need for compliance with obligations arising from promises (as in the last example). However, it would be very difficult to derive any clear set of obligations from the promises above, that was not already in conflict with others yet to come. This is no doubt that this is what makes the design of a Brexit 'solution' so hard to conceive of, for all parties, leading to much evasion about the details by UK politicians. Thinking in promises, on the other hand, may yet prove to be useful in finding a clearer outcome. From promise theory, we know that, while conflicting obligations may lead to paradoxical states, and operational paralysis, conflicting promises merely lead to a manageable question of contexts and partial optimisation of trust.

The example above is only one of many scenarios. One can imagine arguments in favour of Brexit, which do not try to support the four pro Leave promises just mentioned. For instance Minford et.al. 2015 [15] claim that, in the long run, the UK's opt out from adopting the Euro is not tenable for the UK as an EU member. Thus the desire to retain Sterling could be seen as motivating a Brexit.

Indeed there may have been voters who were in favour of Brexit while being unconvinced by the four promises above. If that were shown to be the case, and indeed if the supporters of the four promises were only a minority, then the promise of representing 'the will of the people' (via these four promise criteria) would fail under scrutiny. More specifically, for each of these promises, if it can be shown that the majority of pro Leave voters did not accept that particular promise, at the time of the vote, it is dubious that keeping that promise is even consistent with the intention to follow the will of the people.

In fact, the promise made by voters in the referendum was nowhere close to being able to determine this (see figure 1.1). Hence, trust in UK political representation is the only currently available channel for this information. Future votes and consultations, on specific issues, are another possibility to select a set of majority promises based on a menu of finer grained proposals.

For the purpose of our work it suffices that the relevance of Brexit promises has been established sufficiently well to serve as a motivation for describing the Brexit process with the help of promise theory. The interaction between promises and trust is highly complex, and our objective is not to analyse that interaction in the case of Brexit. We merely intend to survey the past, current, and potential role of promises in connection with Brexit.

1.5.2 Brexit viewed as a UK failure to keep its promises

In Glinavos 2017 [10] the argument is put forward that foreign financial firms might claim to have based investments in the UK on the implicit promise that

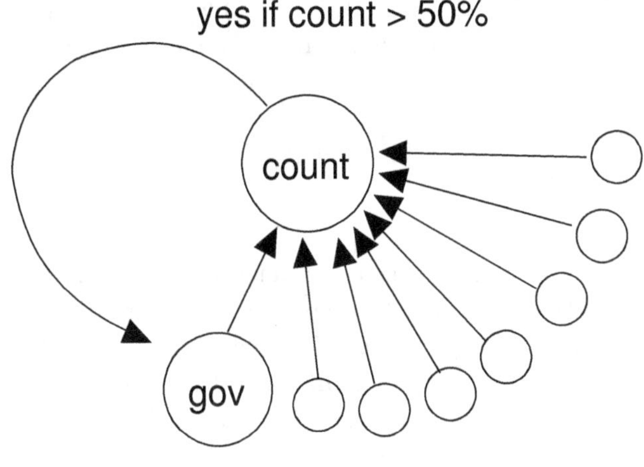

Fig. 1.1.   The referendum voting process was also based on an aggregation of promises by voters to support two referendum options, Leave and Remain, without clarification. If more than half of the votes accepted by the impartial voting authority was in favour of leaving, then, it would promise the government that a result to Leave the EU had been promised by UK citizens. The government's promise to act on this vote was conditional on this, but not a automatic and deterministic fact.

the UK remains within the EU. Should leaving the EU weaken the position of such investors, these investors may raise claims against the UK, and may even try to realise such claims via an appropriate international tribunal.

According to our promise theory, promises do not induce obligations, and although (as stated in [10]) treaties such as the TEU create promises for commercial parties, promise theory does not predict that enforceable obligations arise out of such promises.

1.5.3 Formalisation of the pro Leave promise examples in structured notation

Using the structured notation for promises, a promise issued in advance of the referendum, may be understood as a promise made to an arbitrary prospective voter within the class of UK citizens. Promises tend to support one position or the other (their bias). The second pro Leave promise, mentioned in the previous section, takes the form of a collection of more formal sub-promises, effectively one issued to each individual prospective voter,

> **Promiser.** Prominent pro Leave campaigner.
>
> **Bias.** Pro Leave.
>
> **Type.** [+]
>
> **Body.** There will be no substantial annual financial transfers from the UK to the EU, (unless these transfers constitute contributions made for participation in very specific EU programs such as the famous Erasmus Program). Moreover the UK will be free to direct these transfer streams to different targets (for instance the NHS).
>
> **Condition.** The UK leaves the EU.
>
> **Promisee.** Any prospective referendum voter.
>
> **Scope.** All UK citizens.
>
> **Assessment.** Pending.

We note that the broad nature of the promise makes it difficult to assess a clear outcome. Moreover, it is a promise that may not be finally implemented by those making the promise, thus it is a promise imposed onto someone else to keep, without their consent[7], making it of questionable plausibility, e.g. if there were a change of government. Moreover, each individual recipient or prospective voter may or may not accept the premise of the promise, regardless of its weaknesses.

Accepting the promise can be understood as issuing a corresponding promise to accept (denoted with a minus sign).

> **Promiser.** Any prospective referendum voter.
>
> **Bias.** Neutral.
>
> **Type.** [−]
>
> **Body.** There will be no substantial annual financial transfers from the UK to the EU, (unless these transfers constitute contributions made for participation in very specific EU programs such as the famous Erasmus Program). Moreover the UK will be free to direct these transfer streams to different targets (for instance the NHS).

---

[7] In promise theory, this is a so-called promise of the second kind[1].

Condition. The UK leaves the EU.

Promisee. UK citizen, prospective voter.

Scope. The promiser and other persons with whom they exchange views about this particular promise in advance of the voting.

Assessment. Prominent pro Leave campaigner.

Technically, the issuing of this promise (to accept the campaign promise) has a much smaller scope than the campaign promise itself, so it cannot easily been seen or noticed by anyone. Often, only the promiser, i.e. the voter (not even the promisee, i.e. pro-Leave campaigner), will be in scope of the promise, so the campaigner would be free to speculate about how many in fact noticed and believed in the promise, without factual support. This shows that campaign promises do not normally function as peer reviewable propositions, but only as anchors for blind trust. Furthermore, the limitations of communication and procedure mean that they cannot be supported by a verifiable channel for information exchange.

1.5.4 Preference biases and promises

Besides accumulating promises made on their behalf, a prospective voter will develop a set of preferences. Consider the following abstract version of the mentioned promise to a voter.

Label. Vote Leave as you prefer X.

Promiser. Prominent pro Leave campaigner.

Bias. Pro Leave.

Type. [+]

Body. Future condition X.

Condition. The UK leaves the EU.

Promisee. Any prospective referendum voter.

Scope. All UK citizens.

Assessment. Pending.

In order to conceptualize a prospective voter, we imagine someone who maintains a bundle of preferences or biases regarding the outcome. These preferences may naturally change over time. During a campaign, both sides of the argument convey their preferences or biases in the hope that sufficiently many prospective voters will align with the same preferences. The relation between promises and preferences is thus two-way.

For a person who prefers X over not-X, accepting the promise (labelled 'Vote Leave as you prefer X') brings with it an increased incentive for a pro Leave vote, while for a prospective voter who prefers non-X over X the effect of accepting the same promise is just the other way around. In the case that both leave and remain promises were made, based on the same condition X, voters would tend to maintain their existing bias.

Reasoning backwards, from voting promises to revealed preferences, makes the logic of promises highly non-trivial, even multi-valued. Having promised 'Vote Leave as you prefer X' a vote pro Leave may be construed as revealing a preference for X over non-X. Such reasoning quickly runs into inconsistency if different campaigners make incompatible promises (that is promises which cannot both be kept in the same future). Thus a description in terms of promises is not equivalent to a description of conventional logic, and supports only the simpler narrative about trust.

Preferences may be cast by attaching conditions to promises. When promising 'Vote Leave as you prefer X', implicitly the following promise is conveyed as well.

> **Label.** The better future is with X.
>
> **Promiser.** Prominent pro Leave campaigner.
>
> **Bias.** Pro Leave.
>
> **Type.** [+]
>
> **Body.** A better future for the UK and its citizens, (including the promisee).
>
> **Condition.** Future condition X.
>
> **Promisee.** Any prospective referendum voter.
>
> **Scope.** All UK citizens.
>
> **Assessment.** Pending.

As it stands we are not aware of an unambiguous logic integrating promises and preferences, which might allow one to infer the distribution of voter preferences from the outcome of a vote about the bundles of promises made by either side of the argument. This, in itself, is a significant observation. It means that no rational decision can be made. Once a voting has taken place, all participants are free to bend the reasoning about the relation between promises and preferences towards their chosen political preferences and objectives.

1.6 Promise type qualifiers

A promise qualifier or 'type' informs about two aspects of a promise: (i) whether the promise being issued is in response to another matching promise, and (ii) whether the promiser's forthcoming behaviour, which is the causal factor for keeping the promise, will support the matching promise. The existence of the latter kind of promise is the reason why an agent should not make any promise on behalf of any agent other than itself, since it knows only its own possible behaviours with any certainty, not what may or may not be accepted by another agent. Generally, the more possible freedoms an agent has, the more uncertainty there will be regarding its predictable behaviours. We end up with a number of classes of promise we have use for in what follows:

Documented intention. $+$; promiser claims a causal role in bringing about the expected state of affairs.

These are the promises of the first kind in [1].

Acceptance of documented intention. $-$; promiser accepts the promise ($+$ type) made to it (as a promisee) by an agent (in the role of an original promiser) and renders this acceptance as a promise made to the original promiser.

Rejection of documented intention. $-!$; promiser indicates unwillingness to accept the promise ($+$ type) made to it (as a promisee) and renders this rejection as a promise made to the original promiser.

Documented expectation. $[+]$; promiser claims no causal role in bringing about the expected state of affairs (expectational promise).

These promises correspond to promises of the fourth kind in [1] provided one accepts the existence of an agent which may bring about the expected state of affairs. A documented expectation promise results from a promise of the fourth kind by abstracting from the latter agent. Documented expectations are weaker than documented intentions because the promiser outsources any responsibility for keeping the promise.

Agreement with documented expectation. $[-]$; promiser promises agreement with an expectational promise to the promiser of the latter (acceptance of expectational promise.)

Rejection of documented expectation. $[-!]$; promiser indicates disagreement with original promiser's expectation cast as a promise to the latter (rejection of expectational promise.)

Promise qualifiers are alternatively referred to as promise types.

1.7 Other promise attributes

Besides, promiser, body, promisee, and assessment of outcome, some additional components of promises will be made use of. For instance a promise may be equipped with a label (serving as a name, meant for later reference), a scope, a condition, an event, and a value. A promise may or may not be expired, it may or may not have been kept (outcome assessment). Expiry and assessment may be subjective attributes, in that different agents may disagree about these. Unless stated otherwise, promise expiry and assessment of outcome will be specified from the perspective of the promiser in promise descriptions.

Note finally that promiser and promisee may be clusters and collections of agents (so-called compound agents or 'superagents') rather than individual persons or institutions. Unless self-explanatory these features will be discussed below in more detail.

2

The referendum made binding through promise mechanics

The historic precedent for the 2016 referendum was the 1975 advisory referendum about EC membership, which clearly ended in a positive choice (for membership). The circumstances in 1975 were comparable: it was announced in connection with negotiations about the status of the UK in the EC, and both Labour and Conservatives were split on the matter, including several members of the Labour Cabinet of PM Harald Wilson. In 1972 Norway also had a referendum on EC membership, and subsequently, each time with a negative result.

2.1 The 1974 referendum on EC membership

The referendum as a formalized mechanism with a known process and structure was introduced in the UK in 2000, referendums before that date were arranged in an ad hoc manner. The 1974 Labour manifesto for the upcoming general election introduces the forthcoming referendum as follows.

THE COMMON MARKET

Our genuine concern for democratic rights is in sharp contrast to the Tory attitude. In the greatest single peacetime decision of this century - Britain's membership of the Common Market - the British people were not given a chance to say whether or not they agreed to the terms accepted by the Tory Government. Both the Conservatives and the Liberals have refused to endorse the rights of our people to make their own decision. Only the Labour Party is committed to the right of the men and women of this country to make this unique decision.

> The Labour Government pledges that within twelve months of this election
> we will give the British people the final say, which will be binding on the
> Government - through the ballot box - on whether we accept the terms and
> stay in or reject the terms and come out.

> Labour is an internationalist party and Britain is a European nation. But if
> the Common Market were to mean the creation of a new protectionist bloc,
> or if British membership threatened to impoverish our working people or
> to destroy the authority of Parliament, then Labour could not agree.

> Within one month of coming into office the Labour Government started
> the negotiations promised in our February manifesto on the basis set out in
> that manifesto. It is as yet too early to judge the likely results of the tough
> negotiations which are taking place. But whatever the outcome in Brussels,
> the decision will be taken here by the British people.

The symmetry with the 2015 Conservative manifesto is remarkable: (i) both
Labour and Conservatives are fundamentally split on the subject of EC membership, (ii) the choice between in or out is considered to be of the highest
importance, (iii) new negotiations are announced, the outcome of which will
be judged by a voting, and (iv) the outcome of the voting will be considered
binding. Moreover it is indicated (both by Labour in 1974 and by the Conservatives in 2015) that other parties are disinclined to give the public a say in the
EC membership decision.

When preparing the details of this voting in 1975 it was decided that 50%+1
defines the winning side. When the campaign for the voting started Wilson
came forward with a positive advice (for the UK or remain a member of the EC)
based on his positive assessment of what had been achieved in the negotiations
in Brussels.

When the 2016 referendum would result in the UK remaining in the EU,
not only would the UK be the only EU member at that time to have enjoyed a
positive referendum outcome about the EU, the UK would have collected two
of such outcomes under different governments. All comments on UK loyalty
to the EU would be rendered futile on the spot. It is hard to deny the almost
magical attraction of this possible outcome, and it is easy to sympathize with
PM David Cameron who strove for that opportunity in spite of the undeniable
risk of failure.

Thus, had the 2016 referendum worked out otherwise, the parallel, with the
1975 referendum, with Labour and Conservatives in symmetric roles, would
have been remarkable. However, there was a major difference: in 1975 it would

have been comparatively easy to implement an exit from the EC which the UK had joined only 5 years before in 1970. In 2016, after 41 more years of European integration, the EU and the UK membership of it have grown into a far more complex arrangement from which withdrawal has now become a significantly more challenging task for any UK government, even under optimal conditions with detailed preparation and the frictionless cooperation of all other EU member states.

2.2 2015: manifesto, Queen's Speech, and EU Referendum Act

The Conservative manifesto of 2015[1] in advance of the general election phrases the plan to have a referendum as follows:

> It will be a fundamental principle of a future Conservative Government that membership of the European Union depends on the consent of the British people –and in recent years that consent has worn wafer–thin. That's why, after the election, we will negotiate a new settlement for Britain in Europe, and then ask the British people whether they want to stay in the EU on this reformed basis or leave. David Cameron has committed that he will only lead a government that offers an in-out referendum. We will hold that in-out referendum before the end of 2017 and respect the outcome. So the choice at this election is clear: Labour and the Liberal Democrats won't give you a say over the EU. UKIP can't give you a say. Only the Conservative Party will deliver real change in Europe – and only the Conservatives can and will deliver an in-out referendum. Our plan of action: We will let you decide whether to stay in or leave the EU We will legislate in the first session of the next Parliament for an in-out referendum to be held on Britain?s membership of the EU before the end of 2017. We will negotiate a new settlement for Britain in the EU. And then we will ask the British people whether they want to stay in on this basis, or leave. We will honour the result of the referendum, whatever the outcome.

A subset of the promises contained in the manifesto of the winning party (Conservatives in 2015) made in into the Queen's Speech, and the Queen's Speech of 2015 phrases the upcoming referendum as follows:

---

[1] See e.g. `https://votes4xpatbritsblog.files.wordpress.com/2015/04/conservativemanifesto2015.pdf` for the manifesto.

> My government will renegotiate the United Kingdom's relationship with the European Union and pursue reform of the European Union for the benefit of all member states.

> Alongside this, early legislation will be introduced to provide for an in-out referendum on membership of the European Union before the end of 2017.

There is no confirmation that the referendum will be binding, which leaves open the option that it is advisory, the default status of a referendum in the UK. The subsequent European Union Referendum Act 2015[2] makes no mention of the referendum being advisory or binding.

2.3 Advisory versus binding status of the referendum

Assessing the status of the referendum is non-trivial. Some information on this matter can be found on Full Fact.[3] The referendum is by default supposed to have been advisory, that is not legally binding, which in fact is the status of each referendum in the UK as it has been confirmed by the High Court. In the law that specifies the forthcoming referendum about EU membership it was not stated that either outcome would create a binding obligation for the government to bring about the corresponding state of affairs.

The critical occurrence of the referendum, and of a promise about it which is in excess of the default advisory status of a referendum is in the 2015 Conservative manifesto:

1. In the head-line of a Paragraph it is stated that the in-out decision will be left to the people by means of a referendum. Then it is stated that 'we' will honour the result of the referendum, whatever the outcome. This entails the promise that the referendum will be considered binding for a Government based on a Conservative majority (conditional on the result of the then forthcoming general election).

---

[2] See `http://www.legislation.gov.uk/ukpga/2015/36/pdfs/ukpga_20150036_en.pdf`, 64 pages of detailed regulations, however, without any specification of the meaning or significance of the referendum, and without any specification of a task or responsibility for the Electoral Commission (or any other body or agency) to inform the voters on that matter.

[3] `https://fullfact.org/europe/was-eu-referendum-advisory/` (accessed June 16, 2017).

Obviously an interpretation of this manifesto promise also depends on one's understanding of the concept of a decision. If one understands decision taking in such a manner that a decision to perform action A can be taken and honoured without action A actually being subsequently performed, then taking the decision that the UK will leave the EU can be outsourced to the people of the UK (by the UK Government) by way of a referendum even if it is understood (at the time of taking the decision) that in some realistic scenario's the UK will not leave the EU.

2. It is explained that the Government intends to renegotiate the UK-EU relationship, and subsequently to call a referendum. Clearly at the time of writing of the manifesto PM David Cameron and his cabinet ministers could not know whether or not they were individually going to be pleased with the result of these negotiations. If so they would proceed during the campaign as Remainers, if not they would proceed as campaigning Brexiters. After the vote, they would adapt the outcome.

3. In the main text of the manifesto it is stated that a referendum will be arranged asking to choose between two options: (i) sustained EU membership of the UK under the terms as will have resulted from the announced and forthcoming negotiations, or alternatively (ii) the UK leaves the EU.

4. Remarkably, the alternatives (i) and (ii) just mentioned are not complementary (just as in the 1975 referendum). There is an option in between: rejecting the result of the negotiations while preferring sustained EU membership. The position taken by the manifesto is somewhat extreme because it is implicitly assumed that the outcome of the negotiations will be best possible so that asking for more (concessions from the EU to the UK) would be futile. The negation of (i) is not 'leaving the EU', rather it is disagreement with continued EU membership under the obtained (but not yet known at the time of writing the manifesto) agreement.

5. The question that was asked (yes/no to EU membership) abstracts away from the negotiation outcome altogether. This is an instance of 'take it or leave it' (though both its aren't the same). It is not obvious that having a referendum about UK in the EU or UK outside the EU qualifies as keeping the promise made in the manifesto. By abstracting away from the terms of EU membership in the referendum question there was no incentive either to be specific about the terms of non-membership in the

referendum question, which however is a topic of the highest importance if it actually comes to the process of leaving the EU.

6. In the public opinion as well as in the policies set out by PM Theresa May the Conservative manifesto written in preparation for the 2015 general election stated (promised) that by way of a referendum the decision about EU membership would be left to the people. Now it is not uncommon that a promise contained in a manifesto is not kept by the subsequent government. But by including this particular promise in the manifesto the Conservative Government created first of all the right to proceed with the process of exiting the EU, and secondly a moral obligation for its MPs to support the proposals made to that end, in particular the triggering of Article 50.

7. When viewing the actual referendum question as being quite different from the question as announced (and thereby promised) in the 2015 Conservative manifesto, the referendum as it took place need not be considered an act of keeping a conservative manifesto promise and the idea that the manifesto serves as the basis for overruling the default advisory status of the referendum becomes unconvincing. We conclude that the argument for the binding status of the referendum is unconvincing.

8. In other words: the ambiguity of the Conservative manifesto (announcing an in/out referendum without mention of agreement specifics in summarizing capitals, and announcing a referendum which takes the specifics of the actual agreement that was obtained into account in the subsequent text fragment), plus the absence of any reference to a binding status of the referendum in the 2015 Queen's Speech, and in the subsequent EU referendum Act 2015, makes us disbelieve that voters could or should have known or foreseen that the status of the referendum would in hindsight be portrayed as having been non–advisory.

The general understanding of these matters, however, was as if the Conservative manifesto had announced an in/out referendum without any reference to a particular agreement about the underlying agreement between UK and EU. As a consequence, the outcome of the referendum would then be put into effect, irrespective of views of elected politicians.

The latter promise overrides the underlying general promise that a referendum will be advisory advisory, at least according to the analysis on Full Fact. It follows that a single promise about the status of this particular referendum, made in the Conservative 2015 manifesto, has created the setting in which the conservative MPs could claim not to be obliged to follow their own views on the matter, when voting on the triggering of Article 50. For the Labour MPs there was more freedom but they had to take the fact into account that apparently many Labour voters turned out to vote for Leave. The necessity to take this aspect into account appeared shortly after the triggering of Article 50, when a general election was called unexpectedly (for Labour at least).

The very idea that a single referendum can suffice for taking the decision to leave the EU, as well as for putting that decision into effect, requires further scrutiny given the diversity of scenarios for post-Brexit arrangements between the UK and EU27. At first sight given the complexity of the matter it is quite implausible that a single referendum could possibly reveal the will of the people on how to deal with EU membership.

2.4 Turning the advice of the people into the will of the people

The phrase 'will of the people', as used in when interpreting the outcome of the 2016 referendum, expresses the binding status of the referendum outcome, a binding status which is supposed to be recognized inside as well as outside the group of Conservative MPs. It is obvious that the referendum outcome can be understood as a piece of advice from the people, but turning it into the will of the people, a will which must necessarily be followed by the UK politicians, is a significant further step. For voters who intended to produce an advice, however, it is simply not the case that they intentionally delivered a contribution to the synthesis of a non–negotiable will that must thereafter be pursued whatever the cost.

Here seems to lie a demonstrable weakness of the way in which the referendum has been carried out, the lack of clarity about its advisory status.

2.5 Non–advisory status of the referendum: an incoherent concept?

In terms of promises made by the UK government (that is by PM David Cameron who called for the referendum, when writing the manifesto for the 2015 general election) the referendum question was supposed to be read as follows:

Defiinition 2.5.1 *(UKG-Promise REF-yes) If majority vote = Remain then the UK will remain in the EU.*

Defiinition 2.5.2 *(UKG-Promise REF-no) If majority vote = Leave then the UK will leave the EU.*

Here UKG promises are not to be understood as promises in the sense of promise theory, because UKG promises promises create obligations.[4] As stated above it is unclear to what extent voters understood that the second of these promises might be turned into an unconditional obligation in a matter of weeks.

However plausible this may look, imagine the hypothetical situation in which the UK has become panicked about global warming, and has proposed leaving the Earth in a mass evacuation to the Moon. Hypothetical PM John Waitandsee has lost patience for the debate and has proposed a referendum on the question: 'the UK population will NOT leave the UK for the Moon in the coming 25 years'. Quite unexpectedly the referendum is lost and now John Waitandsee resigns upon allegedly having lost his credibility is succeeded by PM Mary Willofthepeople who (having been a proponent of remaining on Earth in private only and for that reason having lost less credibility with the public at large upon the referendum outcome) takes as a fact that the UK population will indeed be evacuated and be flown to the Moon in the coming 25 years. Unfortunately no detailed plans for this evacuation were made in advance. A secretary for leaving Earth is appointed in order to handle things smoothly.

Obviously a mere referendum outcome plus a promise made by a PM who has not made plans for implementing that particular outcome cannot possibly create a binding obligation for their successor to realise said outcome. This, however, is precisely what seems to have happened with Brexit in the UK. Understanding both referendum outcomes as equally binding appears to be an incoherent idea.

Taking the advice of promise theory into account the negative part of the referendum promise would have been reformulated and modularised, for instance by way of the following combination of promises:

Defiinition 2.5.3 *(UKG-Promise REF-no revised 1.) If majority vote = Leave then the UK will obtain a new government and a new PM who will promise to leave the EU.*

Defiinition 2.5.4 *(UKG-Promise REF-no revised 2.) On a time scale of months the promise to leave the EU by any PM is conditional on the PM having the support of MPs and Lords for that objective, therefore in case of a negative*

---

[4] Actually, promise theory classifies these as promises of another kind, which cannot be kept by the individual making them.

referendum outcome (vote = Leave) new general elections are promised and the conservative manifesto (at least) will promise to work towards withdrawal from the EU.

Defiinition 2.5.5 *(UKG-Promise REF-no revised 3.) Once a strategy for leaving the EU has been detailed, which may take several years of preliminary negotiations with EU27/28, by way of a referendum confirmation will be sought for the second stage of the process including priorities for the follow-up relationship with EU27.*

Moreover the promise to leave the EU by the new government will not create a binding obligation but will create an expectation that the UK proceeds to leave, and will impose on the new government the task to move the UK towards leaving the EU. With renewed self confidence, i.e. not showing amazement at the actual referendum outcome, the hard line Brexiteers should have been keen to frame the referendum as advisory, and to solidify its status. Instead they supported its role in portraying Brexit as a future necessity, probably unaware of the logical problems that such necessities may create.

By portraying Brexit as a necessity it became impossible to even discuss conditions for Brexit, instead the Government promised to accept the even the worst case outcome of forthcoming Brexit negotiations with the EU, that is no progress on any topic at all: crashing out with no deal. By not contemplating possible conditions for Brexit it became plausible to trigger Article 50 without much preparation. That could just as well have been done with a delay of 5 years thereby slowly but steadily forcing EU27/28 to embark on preliminary negotiations about the conditions of leaving the EU, for instance involving a preliminary renegotiation of Article 50.

2.6 Brexiters' lack of self confidence, and its consequences

Proponents of Brexit arguably misunderstood the result of the referendum as creating the necessity of the UK leaving the EU, thereby taking significant control out of the hands of the government. They seem to have failed to grasp that the logical inconsistency, hidden in a non-advisory interpretation of the referendum outcome, itself is a greater risk for its implementation than the risk that a second referendum about EU membership would lead to a different outcome.

After the referendum victory subsequent 'peace negotiations' with their opponents might be in order. During such negotiations the binding interpretation of the result could have been traded for a more predictable process with a high probability, rather than an alleged certainty, of producing a Brexit, by working in a phased manner, possibly involving a second referendum about a major question arising in due time. The binding interpretation (which we claim, is logically incoherent) has forced the government into Article 50[5]

Although it has not been stated clearly in public, the following position might well be held by the current UK government.

Proposition 2.6.1 *'No deal', right from the start (of Brexit negotiations) is better than 'no deal' after two years of uncertainty about the outcome of negotiations.*

Ironically, the strategy chosen by hard line Brexiters seems even to imply a small risk that the UK might ends up adopting the Euro. If delays and uncertainty, together the most powerful weapons in the hands of EU27/28, would prove so harmful for the UK that an escape were needed, and some deeply frustrated EU27 members had it their way, withdrawal of the Article 50 invocation would inflict a high price on the UK: full EU membership without the accumulated prerogatives that the UK has been able to acquire in 40 years of hard-headed negotiation including the Euro–opt–out.

A UK government which is truly empowered (by the people) to execute Brexit would first and for all find out whether or not preliminary renegotiation of Article 50 is needed, a renegotiation which the UK could still push forward as a fully committed EU member. Article 50 creates a grotesquely asymmetric situation, with enormous disadvantages for the member intending to leave. Of course this itself might be held against the EU as one more reason for leaving. However, once adopted as the framework for arriving at Brexit, these disadvantages will show up. Secondly, a precise plan of action (a new set of promises)

---

[5] or, if one disbelieves (or merely disregards) the utterances of several leading conservative politicians, the propaganda for the non–advisory status of the referendum has enabled some remainers within the government, who saw that Brexiters grossly underestimated the technical difficulty of any form of Brexit, to work towards an ill–prepared triggering of Article 50, based negotiations with EU27/28, where the other side is entirely in control of timing and speed. Sheer technical complexity may prove as much of an obstacle for Brexit as it has proven for Republicans in the USA to replace Obama's ACA, in spite of years of promising that this would happen. The republicans, however, have not created a logically incoherent state of affairs, they have merely arrived in a state where (July 2017) they seem to be unable to deliver on a longstanding promise.

on how to proceed after triggering a (possibly) revised Article 50 would be prepared before triggering it.

As it stands, the Brexiters have handed over the task to exit the EU to a PM and a chancellor, both of whom have been low-key remainers prior to the referendum, and who have proven to be fully aware of the hidden inconsistencies lurking in the task.

It strikes us that, at this stage, aborting Article 50, plus redefining the referendum outcome as having been advisory, would have been the safest option from a UK Brexiter point of view. Other policies are likely to become stalled by the built-in paradoxes of the modal logic of obligations. A brief inspection of the complexity of deontic logic ought to suffice for Brexiters (whether trained in formal logic or not) to understand that embarking on such complexities may in fact amount to handing over control to one's opponents.

2.7 The case for a general election in 2017

Below in Section 7.1 we will discuss in detail how an application of the Salisbury Doctrine guaranteed the path to proceed towards triggering article 50, given the Conservative 2015 manifesto and the Conservative majority that resulted from the subsequent general election in 2015 (the change of PM makes no difference on that matter). Moving towards a hard Brexit, however, could not be argued for in the same manner as neither the single market nor the customs union, nor the CJEU are mentioned in the Conservative 2015 manifesto in connection with the referendum announcement.

In order to open the door towards pushing for a hard Brexit right from the start of the Brexit negotiations a government based on an election powered by a new manifesto was needed, in this case a manifesto that is more explicit about an intention of leaving customs union, single market and CJEU. Remarkably calling for new elections could hardly fail to deliver this opening. Either a conservative majority would result which could push forward with a hard Brexit, or in case the conservative majority was lost it was fair to assume that Labour would have opened the door to the various aspects of a hard Brexit in its manifesto (because otherwise it would risk being accused during the campaign of ignoring the will of the people). Thus, in hindsight predictably with a high probability, a majority of MPs would be elected in 2017 on the basis of a manifesto supportive of a hard Brexit, which in fact was the case.

3
Promise mechanism

In this chapter, we review some of the specific technical aspects of promise theory. Although making a promise is an action performed by the promiser it is practical to think of that action as being embedded in a flux of communications between various agents. This interaction might be quite detailed, depending on the level of trust between the agents (see figure 3.1).

Consider a simplified view of these following promise:

Promise label. Offer of delivery of E.

Promiser. *Seller*.

Bias. In favour of the sale of E.

Event. Conversation between *Buyer* and *Seller*, on date d, time t, at the premises of *Seller*.

Type. +

Body. I can deliver you item E within a few days.

Assisting promise. Upon 'purchase of E'.

Promisee. *Buyer*.

Assessment. Pending.

'Sale of E' refers to the following promise (an assisting promise for the offer). According to Bergstra & Burgess [1] an assisting promise is a promise the keeping of which serves as a condition for the assisted promise.

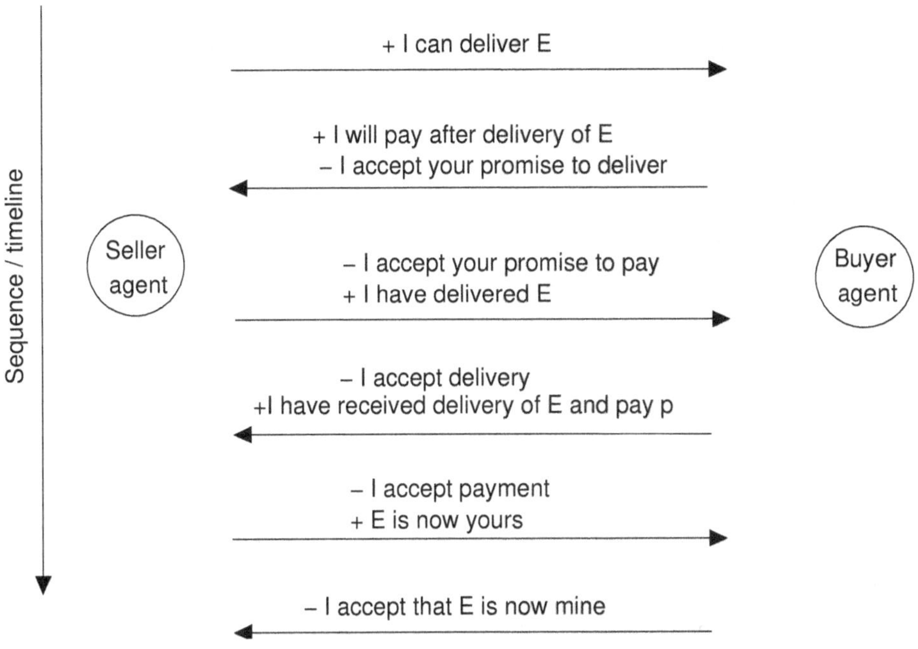

Fig. 3.1. A timeline for buying and selling. When trust is low, each step is verified conditionally. As trust between the parties increases, the number of explicit promises can be simplified.

Promise label. Purchase of E.

Bias. Neutral.

Promiser. *Buyer*.

Event. Conversation between *Buyer* and *Seller*, on date d, time $t + \epsilon$, at the premises of *Seller*.

Type. +

Body. I will buy E and I will pay you EUR p within 10 days.

Condition. Upon delivery of item E.

Promisee. *Seller*.

Assessment. Pending.

Promises often come in pairs. The seller is likely to accept (signalled by –) the promise made by the buyer in terms of and additional promise as follows:

Promise label. Sale of E.

Promiser. *Seller*.

Bias. In favour of the sale of E.

Event. Conversation between *Buyer* and *Seller*, on date d, time $t+\epsilon+\epsilon'$, at the premises of *Seller*.

Type. –

Body. I will sell you E by accepting your payment of EUR p within 10 days after sending you item E, and I will deliver to you item E at my earliest convenience.

Promisee. *Seller*.

Assessment. Pending.

These promises describe the interaction between two agents at some level of abstraction. It is understood that a lot of communication may surround the generation of these promises, for instance *Buyer* may enter the shop, say Hello and be offered a drink by *Seller* and so on.

3.1 Promise context

A promise exists within a certain 'promise context', which specifies all promises and assessments one wishes to take into account in connection with it. Promises move through an evolution in the following sense: as time goes on, the plausibility that agents align with a promise outcome, i.e. the subjective probability that the promise will be kept, may change. Moreover, the assessments that various agents make of the outcome may change too, as agents disagree on whether or not a promise has been kept. In this discussion, all of Brexit related matters will be treated as constituting a single promise context.

3.2 Promise revision and withdrawal

A promiser may revise a promise, e.g. by choosing a better wording for it. A promiser may also withdraw a promise before its expiry. Both revision and withdrawal may modify the trust that the promiser enjoys from other agents in scope of the promise. Promises that are revised frequently typically don't create additional trust, neither does the withdrawal of promises. On the other hand, failure to revise or withdraw a promise in the light of new evidence may generate a loss of trust too, so that an agent may prefer to revise or withdraw a promise assuming that the negative effect on trust will be less.

3.3 Subjective plausibility

At each moment of time, each and every agent assesses the plausibility of an outcome, or default trust in the agent's ability to keep its promises, for any and all promises they know of. This starts with an initial assessment of plausibility or trust, upon receiving the promise, as a result of being an agent in scope. The initial trust, which a promisee assigns to a particular promise outcome, depends on the agent's trust in the promiser itself (perhaps based on past promise keeping, or reputation) as well as the assessor's initial subjective assessment of plausibility for the promise to be issued by a promiser.

Plausibility is subjective in the sense that its assessment may vary from observer to observer. In many cases, the plausibility will be neutral, though in some cases it will be high or low. Plausibility assessments about promises interact with trust assessments about promisers. If many agents assign a low plausibility to promises, issued by some agent A, then in due time the trust in A will degrade, and new promises issued by A will obtain lower initial plausibility. If the promises issued by A gain increasing plausibility, then A's trust level in the perception of other agents will follow suit. Below, the focus will not be on the very complex dynamics of plausibility and trust. The focus will mainly be on promise descriptions.

Assessment (of outcome) is subjective too, but by taking the promiser perspective as a default, the subjectivity of assessment is made less visible.

3.4 Promiser autonomy

As agents, promisers make promises autonomously (or sometimes by proxy). Autonomy is an assumption of the promise theory, as set out in [1]. There is no other penalty, on failure to keep a promise, than the potential loss of trust in the promiser. The keeping promises is not enforced, and there is no concept of obligation used as a conceptual backup for the notion of a promise. Issuing a promise is more like playing a move in a game than like signing a contract.

Indeed binding contracts are stronger than single promises, as they are formed from multiple levels of promises.

A consequence of the promise theory, reported in [1], is the idea that promise theory is simpler than deontic logic (as typically used in law), because promises can't be conflicting in the way obligations can be. As a result, a promiser should not issue a promise on behalf of an entity (agent) which it does not autonomously control, i.e. if it cannot promise without violating the autonomy of another agent. This rule is violated frequently in the context of Brexit promises, and for that reason we will make use of a special qualifier for it: [+].

3.5 Promises in connection with rational social choice

The process of Brexit will have many stages. It is a societal process involving millions of agents, where each citizen of an EU member state counts as an agent, and so do various organisations, institutions, and nations. These agents maintain a matrix of mutual trust.

One way to look at this process is that, in a succession of rounds, the agents involved build up a portfolio of promises (as in figure 3.1). Then, some change (i.e. state transition) takes place, e.g. a referendum, yielding a certain outcome. Following this, the portfolio may be updated, conditional promises may become activated or deactivated, and some promises may be dropped, while all agents update their trust matrices. Then, starting with the promises that have not been dropped, there may be a build up of a new portfolio of promises, until a subsequent state transition takes place, and we start over again. During voting, agents take into account the promises that have been made and the trustworthiness of various promisers.

Suppose that agent A is involved in a voting process concerning the Shakespearian question 'Q or not Q'. If a vote for Q is likely to bring about a state about which a family of promises (conditional upon the outcome of the voting) has been issued by one or more agents, highly trusted by A, and if moreover these promises are assessed positively by A then A may prefer to vote Q rather than not Q.

Best rational voting for A is a matter of (i) balancing trust in one or more agents and the valuation of their promises, (ii) understanding which condition, say C, is more likely to be brought about by voting Q rather than non-Q, and (iii) understanding which of the many promises depend on the condition C. Clearly, rational voting is quite expensive to the voters. They need to assimilate a vast amount of information, which may not be easily available to them, including discovering all the promises they do not know about. There is always uncertainty, because agents cannot know that they have missing knowledge.

A promise to act (+) may induce a counter promise, made by the promisee to accept that action (-). Vice-versa, a promise to accept (-) some action may induce a promise to perform that action (+). The work on promises referred to above provides many examples of that mechanism. In the context of social choice a counter promise may also take the form of a denial of a given promise:

> **Label:** let's go for Q.
>
> **Promiser.** Proponent of Q.
>
> **Bias.** In favour of achieving state Q.
>
> **Type.** [+]
>
> **Body.** Advantage α will come about if option Q is taken.
>
> **Promisee.** Member of Public.
>
> **Assessment.** Pending.

This promise may induce the following one:[1]

> **Label:** let's not go for Q.
>
> **Promiser.** Opponent of Q.
>
> **Bias.** In favour of avoiding state Q.
>
> **Type.** [−!]
>
> **Body.** Advantage α will not come about if option Q is taken.
>
> **Promisee.** Member of Public.
>
> **Assessment.** Pending.

Promises that are not parried by an explicit counter promise may gain plausibility for that very reason. As an indirect consequence of the latter, promisers whose promises are unchallenged (i.e. are not rejected) may gain trust. This has clearly been a mechanism at work in Brexit.

---

[1] There is some discrepancy with the symbolic notation used in [1]. By indicating [−!] as a type it is implied (via −) that the body coincides with the body of a previous promise to which it serves as a counterpart. Via ! it is indicated that the claim implicit in the body is negated. For the sake of readability, but departing from the conventions of [1], the negation is included in the body of the second promise.

3.6 Contexts

In our terminology, state transitions are events which change the state of a system of agents and promises. Upon a state transition, some promises may expire, be assessed as kept or not; similarly, some conditional promises may expire by virtue of their condition being invalidated, or may become unconditional promises by virtue of the condition having become true. It is a matter of taste which events are considered state transitions[2]. From the perspective of promise theory it is profitable to have the stable condition of far fewer state transitions than promises. In a political process, a sustained build-up of a portfolio of promises within its context, happens prior to a vote, the result of which determines a state transition. It is like building a menu of possibilities, from which to choose, or a manual of operations to follow.

State transitions, in this mechanical sense, may fulfill a condition for a promise, turning a conditional promise into one that is simply kept, with an essentially machinelike outcome. This leads to an interpretation of rationality, in which the emotional component has been averaged out (a kind of semantic average), allowing us to argue the case for rational actors. We surely cannot deny that they behave rationally, in the sense of a straightforward change in the contextual constraints, being freed from a conditional promise by turning it into an unconditional promise, or reducing the collection of conditions for the promise.

3.7 Discrete versus continuous state transitions

If new evidence is made available, this fact may also induce agents to revise the plausibility which they assign to various promises, as well as trust they have in other agents. The stream of new information related to a certain topic, ranging from evidence based factual information to so-called 'alternative facts', may be understood as a continuous stream of events, which induces an equally continuous evolution of the promises, within its context.

Besides continuous change, also discontinuous discrete changes take place; for instance, once the outcome of the Brexit vote becomes known. Discrete state transformations may adapt the state in such a manner that conditions for conditional promises become either true (so that the promise into an unconditional phase in its life-cycle) or false (in which the promise is trivially kept and loses its relevance at the same time).

---

[2] For the avoidance of doubt, we use the term 'state' in the sense of a condition or circumstance, i.e. as in information science, not in the meaning of a nation state or government.

3.8 Some discrete state transitions in connection with Brexit

Brexit vote. June 2016 referendum on Brexit, producing a majority for Leave, thereby elevating Brexit to the status of 'will of the people'.

PM switch. Shortly after the referendum David Cameron stepped down as a PM to be succeeded by Theresa May, who also applied a significant reshuffle.

Article 50 vote. The parliament votes (an agrees) on the proposal to trigger Article 50 of the EU treaty.

Article 50 triggering. The act of triggering Article 50 of the EU treaty (March 2017) by way of a letter to that extent sent by PM Theresa may to the president of the EU Donald Tusk.

Forthcoming Brexit agreement. The agreement that finally specifies in detail how Brexit will take place in 2019.

Forthcoming Brexit event. Brexit takes effect (expected in 2019).

3.9 Entities, agents, and agent aggregates

The UK will be negotiating with an EU in state of transition to a new form EU without the UK. The following notation will be used for the various entities.

EU28. EU before Brexit vote and (including UK).

EU27/28. EU minus UK between Brexit vote and Brexit event.

EU27. EU28-UK (= 'EU after Brexit event').

EU. EU28 before Brexit vote, EU27/28 between Brexit vote and Brexit event, EU27 after Forthcoming Brexit event.

The following agents and agent aggregates play a role in the Brexit process.

UK-Gov. UK government.

UK-PM. UK prime minister.

UK-Gov-A, UK-Gov-B,.. UK-Gov members.

UK-Rep. UK representatives, (House of Commons, House of Lords).

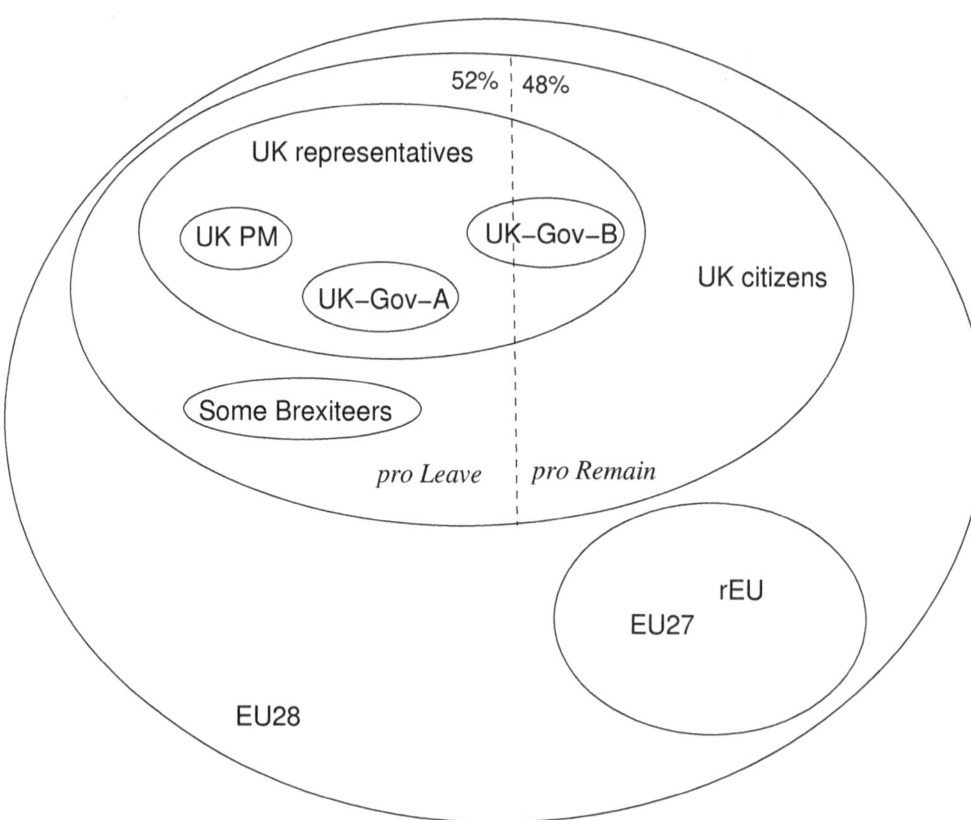

Fig. 3.2. A schematic overview of some of the key agents appearing in Brexit promises, and their relationships to one another.

4

A litany of Brexit related Promises

In this section, we document a number of promises that have been put forward with biases for and against the motion to leave the European Union. It has been remarked that, in a vote between change and no change, the change camp has an automatic advantage in terms of the number and visibility of the promises it can make (regardless of their plausibility). For the case of status quo, there is simply less to say. This may partly account for the claim of the perceived weakness of the Remain campaign, relative to the Leave campaign.

4.1 Promises with a pro Remain bias

The UK remaining in the EU has been denoted 'Remain'. It is informative to imagine which promises might have been put forward under the condition of Remain. Here is a plausible option for such a promise:

Label: Key EU virtues for the UK.

Bias. Pro Remain.

Promiser. Remain proponent.

Type. [+]

Body. Inside the EU the UK will be highly visible within Europe and influential on the world scene because of that influence. The UK is by
now economically thriving within the EU, second to none in terms of
growth, while profiting from being outside the Eurozone, and the UK
will become the most competitive economy in the EU. In terms of

population the UK may well become the largest EU country within several decades, the UK will develop into being the leading economy of the EU.

Promisee. Member of public.

Assessment. Expired (kept by default).

4.1.1 Discrediting potential promises with pro Remain bias

Many promises that could have been be made were likely to be counter productive in terms of attracting voters for the referendum in a Euro-sceptic climate in which many EU projects (e.g. the Euro) are systematically being portrayed as failures beyond repair.

Label: Option to join the Euro.

Promiser. Remain proponent.

Bias. Pro Remain.

Type. [+]

Body. Remaining inside the EU the UK will be be able to join the Euro at any time on advantageous conditions due to its strong economic performance.

Promisee. Member of public.

Assessment. Expired (kept by default).

The following promise capitalises on the Euro becoming a long term success, a position which has been discredited by Brexit proponents, as being one of the reasons for the UK not joining the Euro.

Label: Eurobond market in The City.

Promiser. Remain proponent.

Bias. Pro Remain.

Type. [+]

Body. A significant market for Eurobonds will be developed within the near future as there is no other option for managing the Euro. From within the EU London will be able to play a decisive role in the development of Eurobond trading.

Promisee. Member of public.

Assessment. Expired (kept by default).

The following promise relates to worries about managing the consequences of climate change.

Label: Strong and up to date worldwide position on climate change issues.

Promiser. Remain proponent.

Bias. Pro Remain.

Type. [+]

Body. From within the EU the UK will be able to play a leading role in changing the world economy in ways needed to deal with the problems of global warming as well as with other ecological issues.

Promisee. Member of public.

Assessment. Expired (kept by default).

The EU is likely to expand in coming decades and such developments are quite important for the UK irrespective of whether it is inside or outside the EU. The following promise depends on the expectation that the EU will become yet more strong and inclusive.

Label: Having a say in choosing new EU members.

Promiser. Remain proponent.

Bias. Pro Remain.

Type. [+]

Body. From within the EU the UK will be able to block membership of Turkey, if the UK considers that a wrong development, and the UK will also be able to have decisive influence on a path towards membership for Ukraine.

Assessment. Expired (kept by default).

4.1.2 Project fear was hard to avoid

A difficulty with the promise above, labelled 'Key EU virtues for the UK', is that, if the UK could be the strongest European economy outside the EU, then many voters might prefer that state of affairs. Thus, whatever positive expectation is formulated, against even a light preference for Brexit, such positive expectations do not create a preference for Remain unless it is also promised that (after leaving the EU) these positive expectations will not materialise. Negative promises concerning Brexit take the following form for instance:

Label: Outside the EU the UK GDP will degrade.

Promiser. Remain proponent.

Bias. Pro Remain.

Type. [+]

Body. After leaving the EU, the UK will become less competitive because it will trade with the EU on less favourable terms. This will induce 2% decrease of the GDP.

Assessment. Pending.

Outside the EU the UK (London) based financial industry will mot enjoy passporting rights.

Label: Outside The City will cease to be the financial centre of Europe.

Promiser. Remain proponent.

Bias. Pro Remain.

Type. [+]

Body. After leaving the EU, the financial industry cannot reach out from to EU27 states due to missing passporting rights, as a consequence many companies in the financial sector will need to move.

Assessment. Pending.

Yet another fear that can be turned into a promise is that Brexit will be bad news for the academic system in the UK.

Label: Upon Brexit UK research will miss out on funding from Brussels.

Promiser. Remain proponent.

Bias. Pro Remain.

Type. [+]

Body. After leaving the EU, the financial support from Brussels for research will evaporate. This matters a lot because the UK science is highly competitive and is very effective in project acquisition.

Assessment. Pending.

4.1.3 Pro Remain biased promises: a difficult portfolio design problem

The design of a portfolio of promises, intended to attract voters to a Remain position, faced seemingly unsurmountable difficulties. Its main promise, labelled 'Key EU virtues for the UK', had the disadvantage that it was quite difficult to understand, in practical terms. Why would the expected advantage would come about, and how could that relate to the body of the promise? It seemed to offer only a long term advantage, effected through a lifestyle-like package of behavioural constraints.

The positive promises for EU membership are all problematic in a Eurosceptic context. Each of these promises makes as an assumption that the EU is a living, and potentially very successful, social construction. Most UK citizens would not be in a position to believe this. Finally all disadvantages, phrased as the promise of an expected problem, lack of success, or failure, can be grouped together and subsequently disqualified as constituting one more utterance in 'project fear'. Having grouped all negative predictions (promises) together in an alleged 'project fear', it then suffices to attack only a few of these promises by means of targeted counter promises in order to derail project fear as a whole.

It is attractive to think that the pro Remain arguments are too complex for UK voters to understand, and that taking an informed pro remain position required too much understanding of EU mechanics, with the consequence that this message was also too hard to convey in advance of the referendum. However, the pro Brexit campaign had to deal with a similar problem: the stronger (and more academic) pro Brexit arguments are just hard to convey as those in favour of Remain. It is the long standing erosion of trust in the EU of UK citizens that created an asymmetric setting, in which Brexit proponents had better opportunities for a convincing portfolio of promises.

4.1.4 Pro Remain biased promises in connection with the Brexit process

Brexit, as a social process, has old roots. At some stage the announcement was made to have a referendum on Brexit. This announcement may be understood as a promise made by UK-PM David Cameron, who was in favour of Remain, and quite outspoken about that.

Label: Referendum announcement.

Promiser. David Cameron.

Bias. Pro Remain.

Type. +

Body. There will be a referendum on whether or not the UK ought to be an EU member.

Promisee. UK Parliament.

Assessment. Expired, kept.

And it was indicated that this referendum, although advisory in principle, would have significant impact.

Label: Intended compliance with Brexit vote.

Promiser. David Cameron.

Bias. Pro Remain.

Type. [+]

Body. The UK will leave the EU.

Condition. Brexit vote = leave.

Promisee. UK Public.

Assessment. Pending.

A necessary first step for the UK leaving the EU is a formal notification of this intention to the EU, informally referred to as triggering Brexit.

Label: Initial compliance with Brexit vote.

Promiser. David Cameron.

Bias. Pro Remain.

Type. +

Body. Brexit will be triggered.

Condition. Brexit vote = leave.

Promisee. UK Parliament.

Assessment. Expired, kept.

4.2 Promises with a pro Leave bias

Various pro Leave biased promises may be imagined, which we speculate could have been exchanged in discussions between Brexit proponents and members of public. Some of these would have been undecided, during the process leading up to the referendum. We first describe the basic position of a proponent of Brexit, as it might be put forward, that Brexit would be an option at all. The second and third promise below are about the implementation of Brexit from a UK perspective.

Label: Key Brexit virtues.

Promiser. Brexit proponent.

Bias. Pro Leave.

Type. [+]

Body. Outside the EU the UK will be highly visible on the world scene; about all major parts of life the UK will be able to make up its own mind and to act accordingly. Together these qualities constitute 'freedom'. Freedom is worth a price, for instance a somewhat lower income. For a member of the EU this form of freedom is at best an illusion.

Promisee. Member of public.

Assessment. Pending.

The UK can deliver this desirable state of affairs.

Label: UK civil service competence.

Promiser. Brexit proponent.

Bias. Pro Leave.

Type. [+]

Body. The UK civil service can, in the long run, outperform the services delivered to the UK public from Brussels.

Promisee. Member of public.

Assessment. Pending.

Promise'Brexit unfolding' expresses the expectation that relations between the EU27 and the UK will normalise in due time.

Label: Brexit unfolding.

Promiser. Brexit proponent.

Bias. Pro Leave.

Type. [+]

Body. The EU27 and the UK (after Brexit) will in due course come to a rational agreement which is acceptable for both, and which allows trade to be carried out nearly as efficient as it is today.

Condition. The UK leaves the EU.

Promisee. Member of public.

Assessment. Pending.

4.2.1 Pro Leave arguments not yet cast as promises

Further arguments in favour of Brexit can be advanced. Rather than assigning a truth-value or a probability (expectation value) to each of these arguments, these may be thought of as the bodies for promises, made by an anonymous (and hypothetical) Brexit proponent to a member of public, who might not yet be convinced of Brexit as a good plan.

1. Inside the EU the UK will forever be dominated by Germany which is larger in population and economically stronger.

2. Inside the EU the Pound Sterling will remain of secondary importance only in comparison with the Euro.

3. Outside the EU, the UK is able to protect its own style and ways of working while from inside the EU, the UK will be under the permanent influence and pressure of the bureaucracy which the EU has inherited from the EEC (European Economic Community) and which due to this particular history strongly focuses on EU wide standardisation and formalisation.

4. Outside the EU, the UK will be in control[1] of its own borders and will always be able to determine which foreigners will be allowed to enter the UK and on what basis and for how long they will be permitted to stay in the UK.

---

[1] Here control implies the UK having sole power over who will enter the country and on for how long someone can stay in the UK.

5. In case of hostile relation between the EU and Russia, the UK can (from outside the EU) work as an intermediary party.

6. From outside the EU, the UK can develop and sign appropriate treaties with all states world-wide.

7. The EU is unable to strengthen the national identities of its member states in a systematic and attractive manner.

8. The EU is irreparably fraught by protectionism and clientism (see Minford et al. 2015 [15]). By disassociating itself from those mechanisms the UK will obtain a long term competitive advantage.

9. Remaining inside the EU the UK will on the long run be forced into the Euro and into sustained financial transfer to EU member states with a problematic economy. The flaws of the Euro will sooner or later become a true handicap for the stronger economies in the Eurozone.

10. The EU could have been so much simpler and cheaper. Why does the EU have a Commission at all? If its essence is about trade regulation why not outsource all work done in Brussels to national governments? The build in tendency towards further integration constitutes a risk rather than an advantage.

The promises 'Key Brexit virtues' and 'Brexit unfolding' together with the arguments above describe the case for Brexit in qualitative terms and implicitly determine what it means for Brexit to be a success from a UK point of view.

4.2.2 Brexit related problems with the EU from a UK perspective

From an EU point of view, it is harder to explain at what point Brexit might be considered a success. The central argument in favour of Brexit is stated in Oliver 2013 [18]: Leaving the EU is attractive for those in the UK who don't subscribe the intention of ever closer integration of the EU member states, an ambition which has been built into the EU.[2] Now, Oliver notes a failure within the EU to take this matter seriously, and he expects that this failure will be supportive for the Euro-sceptic positions. The inability of the EU to take UK interests sufficiently into account produces groundwork for the Brexit process. Indeed several difficulties which the UK faces within the EU or may expect to

---

[2] UK-Gov has actually negotiated an opt-out of that ambition in advance of the referendum.

become exposed to on the long run add to a widely felt preference for non-EU membership. Here is an attempt to list such issues.

4.2.3 Moving the Pound Sterling out of the scope of the Euro

It is obvious that the Pound Sterling is not the most important currency in the EU in terms of its widespread acceptance, and that this state of affairs can hardly change. Some nationalists might curiously feel this to be unacceptable for the UK's sovereignty. Thus, only after a Brexit would the UK not be part of an entity within which the GBP was a marginal currency. One can imagine another option: if the 8 other non-Euro area member states of EU27 would have adopted the Pound Sterling as a their currency, the Pound Sterling would become only marginally weaker than the Euro and the EU would host two formidable currencies. However, only a neutrally named currency[3] would ever be acceptable alongside a loss of national sovereignty. The consequences of adopting another nation state's currency is simply too much like conquering, a subject Europeans are still very sensitive about.

> **Label:** The Euro outperforms the Pound Sterling indefinitely.
>
> **Promiser.** $X_{leave}^{EU27/28}$.
>
> **Bias.** Neutral.
>
> **Type.** [+]
>
> **Body.** The Pound Sterling plays a secondary role to the Euro, both inside and outside the EU.
>
> **Condition.** UK remains in the EU.
>
> **Promisee.** C.
>
> **Assessment.** Pending.

By not being a member of the Eurozone of monetary union, the UK finds itself outside of the inner circle of the EU. A naive interpretation of this would claim that this side-lining of the UK is simply a consequence of the UK's opting out of the Euro, but that is only part of the story.

---

[3] Some have claimed that the Euro is not, in fact, neutral, but that it is biased in favour of its historical roots in Germany. However, the name, at least, signifies an inclusive neutrality.

The UK has never indicated any intention to give up the GBP in favour of the Euro. Indeed, cultural differences exist in financialization of the different economies which are generally assumed to explain the desire for Britain to distance itself from the rest of Europe economically. The Eurozone places strong (some have claimed unrealistic) criteria on economic policies of member states for the economic stability of the Euro, which perhaps no member states have observed fully, regardless of their wealth. Since no punitive actions were taken by a central authority, these cannot be regarded as obligations. They were promises, belonging to the treaty, that were not kept. For instance bailing out Greece was not part of the process,[4] and early on both France and Germany ignored bounds on budget deficits that had they had agreed with only a few years before.[5] That behaviour was hard to understand for many EU states, inside and outside the Euro area. (See e.g. Falkner 2013 [9] and Zhang 2017 [22].)

4.2.4 Non-Euro area states as second-class EU members

The result of a tradition of non-compliance with Eurozone promises is that difficulties with the Euro have become far more political than might otherwise have been. Moreover, it left open the historical door to excessive German influence, which was probably even not intended. This goes back to the entry of the UK into the EU. In Eurozone politics, time and again, the economic strength of Germany (as a surplus state) made it more prominent than it would have been without the Eurozone, or with a more stringent enforcement of Maastricht regulations. By accepting Eurobonds, that situation could perhaps have been changed. Thus the UK found itself locked out from a political process which the Maastricht treaty had promised would not exist. Remarkably this observation suggests that a further integration of the Eurozone might have prevented the sentiment of feeling locked out by other countries too. These countries have looked to the UK for support of their situations, as the strongest voice among

---

[4] It is considered by some a weakness of the Maastricht Treaty that there was no canonical solution to the Greek problems, and that political improvisation was needed. However, from a UK point of view one might claim that rather than clever political improvisation, justified by the appearance of extreme circumstances, a renegotiation of the Maastricht Treaty, with the UK as a negotiating party, had been in order.

[5] Speaking in terms of promises: France and Germany have broken promises (of the first kind) as made when adopting the Euro.

them, and have perceived the UK as letting them down by voting for Brexit[6].

Stated differently, the Eurozone has not kept it promises, and by ignoring the promises of intra-Euro area operation it has ignored that in part these were promises with non-Euro area EU member states in scope: i.e.

Label. Maastricht Treaty.

Promiser. Eurozone member states

Event. Signing of Maastricht treaty.

Type. +

Body. The Eurozone member states will comply (regarding Euro management) with Maastricht treaty.

Promisee. Eurozone member states.

Scope. EU member states.

Assessment. Not kept.

This broken promise might be held against the EU and might be considered very costly for the UK indeed. One may imagine that the penalty to be claimed by, and perhaps awarded to, the UK, more than neutralises the so-called exit fee which the UK might be asked to pay to EU27/28 upon Brexit. Stated differently: to what extent are France and Germany at all able to live up to to the agreements they have signed. The EU as an institution is expected to create and demonstrate new levels of mutual trusts after three consecutive wars between France and Germany within the time span of 75 years. Although the EU has contributed greatly to increased mutual trust the problematic history of the Euro has nevertheless may have lowered trust.[7]

4.2.5 Unfair treatment under formally agreed opt-outs

What may have been frustrating for some in the UK, is that the Eurozone has by now adopted, in practice if not in theory, a tradition of ad hoc and informal non-compliance by its member states, whereas the UK negotiates in detail, and

---

[6] This is where one could argue a moral duty of Britain to remain in the EU as a leader and magnanimous advocate for less powerful nations.

[7] Perhaps including the Chair of the BoE as a permanent member of the ECB board, equipped with a relatively low right regarding voting frequency, could have solved this difficulty with regard to the UK.

to completion, about each and every form of non-compliance with EU regulations it wishes to be permitted. In other words, the opt-outs which the UK has achieved mean much less than one might hope in the light of the fact that the Eurozone has (almost from day one) become an implicit non-agreed opt-out permissive area for France and Germany zone.

4.2.6 Creating more equality at a lower average income level

According to Beunder 2016 [2], the outcome of the the Brexit vote can be understood as an application of the Stolper–Samuelson model for the free interaction between two economic entities, with different distribution of competence levels, in the respective populations. One can imagine that by drastically reducing the influx of foreign workers lower incomes will be raised, while middle and higher incomes drop. In this manner the voters who (unknowingly) followed the Stolper–Samuelson logic may find themselves in an improved situation even if, for the UK as a whole, the average income decreases as a consequence of Brexit.

Kaufman 2016 [11] provides an entirely different analysis of the correlation between Brexit voting and other measurable properties of voters. Kaufman concludes that economic aspects have been less important than cultural aspects, in particular (in my own words) 'an outspoken law and order attitude' would correlate highly with pro Leave voting.

4.2.7 English as a lingua Franca and the consequences thereof

Mainly because of the Americanization of the world, in the post world war period, very many in the EU (and beyond) are exposed to English courses. In practice, English is the most ubiquitous language within the EU, and it is the language of international commerce. It is often used as a preferred joint language for persons from different language backgrounds.

This must bias the desire for migration to the UK, as an option for EU27/28 citizens, far more so than the other way around. Requiring the UK to welcome persons of other EU27 states in a manner symmetric with how other EU27 member states welcome UK citizens is perhaps treating unequal parties equally, in a way which is unfair to the UK. In other words, perhaps the UK ought to be entitled to some additional barriers against incoming EU27 citizens.

4.2.8 The will of the people counts in the UK

Does it matter that a majority of only 52% over 48% voted in favour of Brexit?
And does it matter that the preceding campaign saw many false statements
made. It matters if one's view of democracy is that the majority vote is an
outcome of rational deliberation, or perhaps an outcome of the discernible desire of the people. Majority voting can have different faces, however; it may
in some cases express a clear and unambiguous sentiment, but it in other cases
majority voting may turn out to be rather random. In the Brexit case it could
have gone either way.[8] It is probably a strength of democracies that random
flips of decision of this kind (stochastic state transitions) take place every now
and then. So, instead of being worried that Brexit vote might have ended up
differently (had the problematic claim about rerouting money from EU to the
NHS not been made), it would be more convincing to agree that, in advance of
the voting, either outcome was possible, and that the actual vote was no more
than a random outcome. It is taken very seriously nonetheless, on the principled
and hallowed grounds of democratic process. Given the long stalemate regarding Brexit or Remain it might have been equally reasonable to toss a coin, since
that in effect is what actually took place. It could have gone either way. But the
UK has demonstrated not being afraid to put the most significant choices in the
hands of the voters.

4.2.9 EU27/28 negotiation planning, a possible source of frustration

It seems that the burden of demonstrating the feasibility of Brexit has been
shifted entirely onto the UK, placing the UK at a disadvantage. In a blue eyed
view, where politics are for the good of the people, the EU27/28 might better
have promised the UK (or any other member state) a clear and workable way
out, right from the start. Such an exit mechanism could have been known to
all voters in advance of the June 2016 referendum in the UK. Indignation about
Brexit, by EU27, is not righteous, and the political posturing on both sides has
devolved almost into a surrogate conflict, thus far only in words.

Thus a referendum, or some form of general voting, is supposedly needed in
advance of triggering Article 50. Different readings of that article have been
given. Moreover, because negotiations can start only after triggering Article 50,
it could be argued that it was simply impossible for David Cameron to phrase

---

[8] In Low 2016 [13] it is argued that the outcome did not align with the will of the people, and
is better looked at as no more than an artefact of a debatable voting procedure.

the question for the referendum more clearly than was actually the case (should I stay, or should I go?).

The idea that EU27/28 can single-handedly impose an agenda for Brexit negotiations is counter-intuitive, and so is the idea that the European commission represents EU27/28. The UK still owns shares in the European Commission and thus it should (at least for that part) support the UK. Together these factors may constitute a source of frustration for Brexit proponents in the UK. A well-prepared exit mechanism ought to exist for the EU as well as for the Eurozone.

EU27/28 has now promised not to negotiate on trade relations after Brexit until a series of issues have been successfully dealt with first. By working this way, they extend the period that the UK government cannot explain the UK population what to expect in terms of subsequent trade agreements. In the absence of any convincing and predictable exit mechanism it is plausible that Brexit proponents in the UK will develop a sense of urgency as every year of delay of Brexit makes departure from the EU harder.

Systemically, from the perspective of systemic reliability and safety, it would seem more appropriate if the negotiations would proceed in three phases: first a backdoor exit deal is designed: that is a deal which is already better than no deal, and then the EU27/28 priorities (exit fee, status of UK residents with an EU27 nationality, status of UK citizens living in UK27 states) are dealt with, so that in a final round the trade agreements can be reconsidered with the intention to design a better agreement for all parties, if possible.

It seems that the TEU makes exit from the EU for any member state cumbersome, unpredictable, and unnecessarily risky, with a far too large role played by negotiations between the UK and the EU27/28

4.3 Cherry picking and its ramifications

Several EU27/28 politicians have promised not to accept so-called cherry picking by the UK. Cherry picking amounts to insisting on a trade agreement replacing EU membership after the UK has left the EU, which contains only those features which the UK deems useful for its own objectives. From a pro Leave standpoint the matter may be captured in terms of promises as follows:

Promiser. UK-Gov.

Bias. Pro Leave.

Type. [+]

Body. Each state exiting from the EU (the UK may just be the first case
after all) will need tailor made agreement for the period thereafter.

Promisee. EU27/28.

Scope. EU citizens.

Assessment. Pending.

Labelling this promise as an unreasonable claim, made from within the UK, on
some right of arbitrary cherry picking is nonsensical. The following promises
indicate why.

Promiser. UK-Gov.

Bias. Pro Leave.

Type. [+]

Body. Each EU member state will always appreciate the possibility to exit
from the EU on workable terms, and such terms cannot be set in stone
in advance.

Promisee. EU27/28.

Scope. EU citizens.

Assessment. Pending.

Indeed if cherry picking is denied to the UK as a matter of principle by EU27/28
then it should be denied in every subsequent case of a country leaving the EU.
Finally UK-Gov expects that some form of cherry picking will be accommo-
dated for the simple reason that doing so is in the interest of EU27/28.

Promiser. UK-Gov.

Bias. Pro Leave.

Type. [+]

Body. Attractive options exist for a forthcoming UK-EU27 trade agreements which lie between the Norway option and the Canada option.
UK-Gov will make a best possible attempt to achieve such an follow-
up treaty.

Promisee. EU27/28.

Scope. EU citizens.

Assessment. Pending.

4.3.1 More pro Leave biased promises

1. **Label:** Brexit is Brexit.

   Promiser. UK-Gov.

   Bias. Pro Leave.

   Event. Frequent public announcements.

   Type. +

   Body. Brexit will be put into effect.

   Promisee. UK-citizens.

   Scope. EU citizens.

   Assessment. Positive.

2. **Label:** Better no deal than a bad deal.

   Promiser. UK-Gov.

   Bias. Pro Leave.

   Event. Frequent public announcements by PM Theresa May.

   Type. +

   Body. Brexit will be put into effect, even if no attractive deal can be negotiated.

   Promisee. UK-citizens.

   Scope. EU citizens.

   Assessment. Pending.

3. **Label:** Brexit will be made a success.

   Promiser. UK-Gov.

   Bias. Pro Leave.

   Event. Frequent public announcements.

   Type. [+]

Body. Brexit will be considered to constitute a step forward for the UK.

Condition. The UK leaves the EU.

Promisee. UK-citizens.

Scope. EU citizens.

Assessment. Pending.

4. **Label:** Parliamentary vote on Article 50 triggering.

   Promiser. UK-Gov.

   Bias. Pro Leave.

   Event. Letter to the parliament.

   Type. +

   Body. Before Brexit is triggered parliament will be allowed to have a vote on that matter.

   Promisee. UK MEPs.

   Scope. UK citizens.

   Assessment. Pending.

5. **Label:** No second referendum.

   Promiser. UK-Gov.

   Bias. Pro Leave.

   Event. Public announcements.

   Type. [+]

   Body. There will not be a second referendum on Brexit versus Remain, and neither will there be a referendum on the final conditions of Brexit.

   Promisee. UK MEPs.

   Scope. UK citizens.

   Assessment. Pending.

6. **Label:** Car industry protection.

   Promiser. UK-Gov.

   Bias. Pro Leave.

Event. Press release.

Type. +

Body. Nissan will be able to run its UK based car production after Brexit under comparable conditions as before.

Promisee. Nissan management.

Scope. All UK citizens.

Assessment. Pending.

4.4 Miscellaneous promises in connection with Brexit

After the referendum (resulting in Leave), the advisory status of the referendum made a subsequent political process necessary, in order to determine whether or not Brexit was actually going to happen. The pro Leave and pro Remain biases were in place, until the Article 50 vote marked the change to a state in which Brexit was committed to. Following this, a pro Leave bias might be considered meaningless. The following promises were relevant until the Article 50 vote took place.

1. The following promise sounds like a tautology, if one defines 'a bad deal' as a deal which is inferior to 'no deal'. But that is not the intended meaning, a bad deal is understood as a deal which is not clearly a good deal. This kind of promise has no manifest bias.

   Label: No deal is better than a bad deal.

   Promiser. UK-Gov.

   Bias. pro Leave.

   Type. +

   Body. If negotiations with the EU are too difficult, 'walking away, that is a hard Brexit' is an option.

   Promisee. UK-citizens.

   Scope. EU citizens.

   Assessment. Pending.

2. **Label:** Exit from ECHR.

   Promiser. UK-Gov.

   Bias. pro Leave.

   Event. Public announcements.

   Type. +

   Body. The UK will leave the ECHR (European Convention of Human Rights).

   Promisee. UK-citizens.

   Scope. EU citizens.

   Assessment. Pending.

3. **Label:** Exit from ECJ.

   Promiser. UK-Gov.

   Bias. pro Leave.

   Event. Press release.

   Type. +

   Body. Upon Brexit the UK will also withdraw from the ECJ (European Court of Justice).

   Promisee. UK citizens.

   Scope. EU citizens.

   Assessment. Pending.

4. **Label:** Euratom departure.

   Promiser. UK-Gov.

   Bias. pro Leave.

   Event. Press release.

   Type. +

   Body. The UK will withdraw from Euratom.

   Promisee. UK nuclear industry.

   Scope. All UK citizens.

   Assessment. Pending.

5. **Label:** Euratom departure warning.

   Promiser. UK nuclear industry managers.

   Bias. neutral.

   Event. Press release.

   Type. [–!]

   Body. The UK cannot withdraw from Euratom unless alternative structures and agreements are in place; uncertainty about these matters creates an acute problem.

   Promisee. UK Gov.

   Scope. All UK citizens.

   Assessment. Pending.

6. **Label:** 350 M for NHS.

   Promiser. Pro leave campaign.

   Bias. pro Leave.

   Event. Visual display on campaign bus.

   Type. [+]

   Body. The 350 million Pound which is weekly transferred to the EU will be rerouted to the NHS.

   Promisee. All UK citizens.

   Scope. All UK citizens.

   Assessment. Pending.

This promise was implicit from texts on the Vote Leave campaign bus. On the Vote Leave site the NHS was merely mentioned as a possible destination of the same money stream. The assertion amounts to (i) promising that the business case of Brexit will be positive to such an extent that the regular allotment to the EU can be rerouted, and (ii) estimating the latter amount at £ 350 million each week.

Many similar promises are known to have been targeted closely to finely grained voter groups, such as fishing communities, through social media channels like Facebook campaigns.

7. **Label:** Twofold 350 M for NHS denial.

   Promiser. Pro remain campaign.

   Bias. pro Remain.

   Event. Repeated statements in public.

   Type. [-!]

   Body. Only 250 million Pound is weekly transferred by the UK to the EU. And these transfers come with advantages that may be lost with a hard Brexit, or must be compensated for by means of comparable payments.

   Promisee. All UK citizens.

   Scope. All UK citizens.

   Assessment. Pending.

8. **Label:** Quick downturn upon an exit outcome of the Brexit vote.

   Promiser. Bank of England (BoE).

   Bias. neutral.

   Type. [+]

   Body. There will be a rather sudden downturn in the property market as well as in the UK economy as a whole once the Brexit vote outcome predicts that Brexit will become a fact.

   Promisee. All UK citizens.

   Scope. All EU citizens.

   Assessment. Negative, the UK economy has been thriving throughout 2016 and the first months of 2017.

9. **Label:** Slow downturn upon an exit outcome of the Brexit vote.

   Promiser. BoE.

   Bias. neutral.

   Event. Repeated statements in public.

   Type. [+]

   Body. There will be a downturn in the property market as well as in the UK economy as a whole once the Brexit vote outcome predicts that the UK will leave the EU, this downturn will mainly be felt in the 3 years after the Brexit vote.

Promisee. All UK citizens.

Scope. All EU citizens.

Assessment. Pending.

10. **Label:** UK exit payment.

    Promiser. EU27 politicians.

    Bias. neutral.

    Type. +

    Body. The UK will pay a substantial amount (exit fee) corresponding to its share in recent financial commitments of the EU taken on board while the UK was a member.

    Promisee. All UK citizens.

    Scope. All EU citizens.

    Assessment. Pending.

11. **Label:** UK exit payment rejection.

    Responding to: UK exit payment promise.

    Promiser. Some UK politicians.

    Bias. Pro Brexit

    Event. Repeated statements in public.

    Type. −!

    Body. The UK will not accept a claim from the EU for an exit fee. taken on board while the UK was a member.

    Promisee. European Commission.

    Scope. All UK citizens.

    Assessment. Pending.

12. **Label:** UK exit payment warning.

    Responding to: UK exit payment promise.

    Promiser. UK-Gov Brexit minister.

    Bias. Pro Leave.

    Type. −!

    Body. The UK will not accept a claim from the EU for an exit fee in excess of 100.000.000 Euro.

    Promisee. European Commission.

    Scope. All UK citizens.

    Assessment. Pending.

    Passporting rights are a phrase used to describe a mechanism for providing financial industry based in one EU member state access to the market of financial services in other member states.

13. **Label:** Loss of passporting rights.

    Promiser. EU commission.

    Bias. Neutral.

    Event. Public statement.

    Type. [+]

    Body. UK financial institutions (including non-EU financial institutions working in the EU) from the UK will lose passporting rights.

    Promisee. UK based financial institutions.

    Scope. EU citizens.

    Assessment. Pending.

14. **Label:** Euro clearing inside EU.

    Promiser. EU commission.

    Bias. Neutral.

    Type. [+]

    Body. Euro clearing will be moved into one or more EU member states.

    Condition. UK leaves the EU.

    Promisee. UK citizens.

Scope. EU citizens.

Assessment. Pending.

15. **Label:** Euro clearing will stay in the City.

    Promiser. Financial experts in London.

    Bias. Neutral.

    Type. [+]

    Body. If Euro clearing is moved out of London there will be significant financial instability throughout the EU27, and there will be much higher financing costs to EU27 member states and the activities carried out in these states.

    Promisee. UK citizens.

    Scope. EU citizens.

    Assessment. Pending.

16. **Label:** Car industry needs more than WTO.

    Promiser. LSE economists.

    Bias. Neutral.

    Type. [+]

    Body. Upon a hard Brexit (walking out into the WTO system of regulations), the UK based car industry will be in trouble.

    Promisee. UK Gov.

    Scope. UK citizens.

    Assessment. Pending.

5

The evolution of bias issues

Promise biases, which emerge in connection with a referendum or an election, may plausibly be viewed as coming in complementary pairs. In an ideal world, this would be an oversimplification, but in contemporary political systems it is a natural and deliberate polarization. Leave versus Remain is the bias pair which has dominated the discussion, within the UK, in the process leading to the referendum in 2016.

The promises, which have been issued in public space, in connection with Brexit and before the referendum, were mostly either Pro Leave biased or pro Remain biased. Such promises made sense until the Article 50 vote took place. Thereafter the opposing bias pair became hard Brexit versus soft Brexit. At first sight, achieving a hard Brexit (crashing out) might seem to be a clear state of affairs, but nontrivial negotiations would still be needed in order to disconnect the UK from the EU. The rights and prerogatives that the EU has carved out for itself within the WTO, for instance in connection with agricultural subsidies, must be somehow split in two parts.

We will refer to this interpretation of a hard Brexit as WTO Brexit. Soft Brexit, when defined, as 'not a hard Brexit', is a less clear concept. The softest form of Brexit that has been widely discussed is termed the 'Norway option' and would imply that the UK joins the EEA, or that a very similar arrangement is agreed. We will refer to this option as the EEA Brexit. Many forms in between may be imagined.

5.1 From Leave versus Remain, to Tory Leave versus Tory Remain

After the Article 50 vote, the dominant bias pair evolved from being 'Leave vs Remain' to being 'Hard Brexit vs Soft Brexit'. Remarkably, once Theresa May announced a general election for June 2017 the most dominant bias pair became: UK-PM remains in place (Tory Remain) or UK-PM leaves in favour of a government led by Labour (Tory Leave, i.e. no Conservative PM in Downing street 10).

The 'Pro Tory Remain vs Pro Tory Leave' bias pair is likely to be replaced soon, having become rather obsolete after the June 2017 elections. Here are some promises with either Pro Tory Remain or Pro Tory Leave as a bias that were used in the course of the election campaign:

Label: The conservatives can handle Brexit.

Promiser. Theresa May (conservative).

Bias. Pro Tory Remain.

Type. +

Body. Negotiations triggering Article 50 will be complex. I will perform well in Brexit negotiations with EU27/28.

Promisee. UK voters.

Scope. UK voters.

Assessment. Pending.

Rather personal attacks on the shadow PM (Jeremy Corbyn) were phrased in terms of promises.

Label: The Jeremy Corbyn cannot handle Brexit.

Promiser. Theresa May.

Bias. Pro Tory Remain.

Type. +

Body. Negotiations on the terms of Brexit will be complex. A Labour led government will perform badly in Brexit negotiations with EU27/28.

Promisee. UK voters.

Scope. UK voters.

Assessment. Pending.

Even more generally:

> **Label:** Labour cannot handle Brexit.
>
> **Promiser.** Theresa May.
>
> **Bias.** Pro Tory Remain.
>
> **Type.** +
>
> **Body.** Negotiations on the terms of Brexit will be complex. A Labour led government will perform badly in Brexit negotiations with EU27/28.
>
> **Promisee.** UK voters.
>
> **Scope.** UK voters.
>
> **Assessment.** Pending.

From the opposite side (Tory Leave Bias) opposite promises are issued.

> **Label:** Labour can handle Brexit.
>
> **Promiser.** Jeremy Corbyn.
>
> **Bias.** Pro Tory Leave.
>
> **Type.** +
>
> **Body.** WTO Brexit is not a successful Brexit. I will achieve a better Brexit than a hard (that is not a WTO Brexit, the so-called no deal Brexit).
>
> **Promisee.** UK voters.
>
> **Scope.** UK voters.
>
> **Assessment.** Pending.

and,

> **Label:** The Labour candidate PM can and will adequately handle Brexit.
>
> **Promiser.** Jeremy Corbyn.
>
> **Bias.** Pro Tory Leave.
>
> **Type.** +
>
> **Body.** Negotiations on the terms of Brexit will be complex. I will perform well in Brexit negotiations with EU27/28.
>
> **Promisee.** UK voters.
>
> **Scope.** UK voters.

Assessment. Pending.

Remarkable promises have been made in advance of the June 2017 election, for instance:

Label: Fox hunting reconsidered.

Promiser. Theresa May.

Bias. Pro Tory Remain.

Type. +

Body. Fox hunting will be re-legalised.

Condition. Tories Remain in power.

Promisee. Minority of UK voters (fox hunting enthusiasts).

Scope. UK voters.

Assessment. Pending.

Promise theory suggest that the latter promise was made as an olive branch to build the trust amongst a select group of British society. It seems implausible to us, however: that minority, pleased with a renewed perspective on fox hunting, would know quite well that going public with such a promise risked losing the trust of far more potential conservative voters, as well as the risk of activating a sleeping opposition.

Some promises are made in order to frame a promise made by other agents in an unfavourable light (a network interference effect), for example:

Label: No dementia tax.

Promiser. Jeremy Corbyn.

Bias. Pro Tory Leave.

Type. +

Body. A labour government will not implement the so-called dementia tax as proposed by the Conservatives.

Condition. Labour wins the election.

Promisee. UK voters.

Scope. UK voters.

Assessment. Pending.

5.2 Non-WTO Brexit with or without EFTA membership

The question of what kind of membership might replace EU membership, for the UK, is discussed in detail by Dhigra & Sampson 2016 [5]. It was concluded that re-joining EFTA would not satisfy the needs of the UK. Indeed, each of the four EFTA members has additional arrangements (Norway, Iceland and Liechtenstein are members of EEA, along side EU member states), whereas Switzerland maintains a portfolio of bilateral agreements with the EU. The issue may be captured in terms of promises as follows:

Label: UK to join EFTA after Brexit.

Promiser. Some Brexiters.

Bias. Pro non-WTO Brexit.

Event. Public statements.

Type. [+]

Body. After Brexit the UK will join EFTA.

Promisee. UK citizens.

Scope. EU citizens.

Assessment. Pending.

Label: UK not to join EFTA after Brexit.

Promiser. EFTA management.

Bias. Neutral.

Event. Public statement.

Type. -

Body. EFTA is unlikely to welcome the UK after Brexit.

Promisee. EFTA member citizens.

Scope. UK citizens.

Assessment. Pending.

Promises concerning EFTA are somewhat confusing. The following promise replaces rather than rejects 'UK not to join EFTA after Brexit.'

Label: UK not expected to join EFTA after Brexit.

Promiser. EFTA management.

Event. Public statement.

Bias. Neutral.

Type. [-]

Body. The UK will not enter EFTA after Brexit (because the UK said no thank you).

Promisee. EFTA member citizens.

Scope. UK citizens.

Assessment. Pending.

5.3 WTO Brexit versus non-WTO Brexit: the benefits of having a few EU institutions

Whoever is in charge after the June 2017 elections, the subsequent bias pair for forthcoming promises will initially be 'WTO Brexit vs non-WTO Brexit'. Once negotiations proceed, and achieving a softer Brexit than WTO Brexit becomes more likely, a more refined terminology concerning promises biases will emerge. Many other bias pairs can be imagined: EFTA Brexit versus non-EFTA Brexit, single market Brexit versus non-single market Brexit, Customs Union Brexit versus non Customs Union Brexit. However, each of these bias pairs are missing the seemingly clear dichotomy of (EU) Leave versus (EU) Remain.

Questions remain even with the WTO Brexit option: will the UK leave the Euratom Treaty (nuclear cooperation and compliance), will it still participate in the European Convention on Human Rights (ECHR)? Will the UK still participate in specific programs for science and research? It appears that a WTO Brexit, widely acknowledged as the simplest option around, is still a very complex arrangement which requires many difficult choices to be made.

In hindsight, the following question arises: would it have been productive for the UK first to require the EU to reform itself, i.e. to reform the Lisbon Treaty itself, so as to prepare for an more orderly exit and only then to strive towards Brexit. Some kind of general exit baseline, far more detailed than Article 50 could have been agreed.

Obviously the referendum voters in the UK, at the time of the referendum, could not have had a clear view of what is involved even for the most straightforward implementation of Brexit. In spite of its simple appearance reading Article 50 requires much legal knowledge, as emerges from Eeckhout & Frantziou

2016 [8]. Although all voters could have known in advance of the referendum that leaving the EU would imply the use of Article 50 in some stage, few if any may have grasped what that actually means. In [8] the following promise is made:

Label: The UK may (when done in a bona fide manner) withdraw from the announcement that it will leave the UK within 2 years after 'triggering'.

Promiser. authors of [8].

Bias. Neutral.

Type. [+][1]

Body. The UK may withdraw from its unilateral decision to leave the EU within the time frame of two years after the notification of its intent.

Condition. (i) Article 50 negotiations not yet terminated, and (ii) there is new and relevant information that the UK people has changed its mind on the desirability of Brexit.

Scope. UK citizens.

Assessment. Pending.

The view underlying this promise transpires also from Rampen 2017 [21].

Label: The right time for transition is now.

Promiser. EU Brexit negotiator.

Bias. Pro non WTO-Brexit.

Type. [+]

Body. The UK will leave the EU, the coming 1.5 years provide the time for business and industry to adapt to this new reality, even if some aspects of the future circumstances are not known. (Waiting with actions in anticipation of Brexit until an agreement has been found in expectation of a transitional phase is not advised.)

Promisee. EU business leaders.

Scope. EU citizens.

Assessment. Pending.

---

[1] This is a conditional promise of the second kind in the classification of [1]. The promise is made on behalf of UK-Gov.

5.4 Transition deal or no transition deal

In July 2017, it became clear that the details of leaving the EU could not possibly be laid down within two years. A new polarization appeared between the promises made and the stated preferences: must the UK try to steer negotiations towards an extended transition period, during which the UK complies with EAA regulations (in advance of leaving both customs union and single market) or not?

At the end of July 2017 it appeared that the UK Government (minus the PM who was on vacation in the Alps) was unanimously thinking in terms of a transition period. By articulating a preference for a transition period, the slogan 'better no deal than a bad deal' seemed contradicted (assuming one takes no-deal to mean the exiting from the EU in the absence of an agreed deal).

6

Making Brexit a success

Although it currently seems controversial (if not actually perverse) to suggest it, Brexit could be portrayed as a potential success for EU27/28. it could be framed as a showcase for the principles and processes of European freedom and democracy—something that would be quite impossible in almost any other region of the world. Once the promise that the UK will leave the EU is accepted, there is no further reason or need for the UK to analyse the fracture in terms of the objectives of those who pushed for it. As a development within Europe, it can be analysed from all perspectives, and the calculus of advantages is not owned solely by its advocates, just as the calculus of its disadvantages is not owned by its opponents.

6.1 Potential advantages of Brexit for EU27/28 members

Potential successes, arising from the UK leaving the EU, from the perspective of the EU27/28, may have diverse forms, some of which are listed here. Each of these motives may be wrapped in a (possibly hypothetical) promise issued by a hypothetical analyst $X_{leave}^{EU27/28}$, who contemplates how to make the best out of Brexit for EU27/28 at the EU27/28 side to an arbitrary citizen C of an EU27/28 member state. Promise bodies are stated in terms of EU27, because these refer to the state of the EU after Forthcoming Brexit event.

1. The EU economic activity understood as a yield per member state may develop with more strength than the corresponding developments would have been (per member state) within an EU28, mainly due to the transfer of profitable activities from the UK to the remaining states.

> **Label:** Transfer of activity from UK to EU27.
>
> **Promiser.** $X_{leave}^{EU27/28}$.
>
> **Bias.** Neutral.
>
> **Type.** [+]
>
> **Body.** Significant economic activity is transferred from the UK to EU27, in particular in the financial industry, in car manufacturing, an in the pharmaceutical and chemical industry.
>
> **Condition.** UK leaves the EU.
>
> **Promisee.** C.
>
> **Assessment.** Pending.

2. By being reduced in size and strength in the West, the EU may well be in a better position to grow in Eastern direction. Inclusion of additional states from Eastern Europe has the potential of becoming a successful direction of development for the EU.

> **Label:** EU27 expanding Eastward.
>
> **Promiser.** $X_{leave}^{EU27/28}$.
>
> **Bias.** Neutral.
>
> **Type.** [+]
>
> **Body.** EU27 will expand with one or more additional member states from Eastern Europe.
>
> **Condition.** UK leaves the EU.
>
> **Promisee.** C.
>
> **Assessment.** Pending.

3. An EU reduced in size (from EU28 to EU27) is more effective in decision making, simply because it is smaller, while its decisions may well have the same (and thus in relative terms even more) impact.

Label: Policy outreach of EU almost unaffected.

Promiser. $X_{leave}^{EU27/28}$.

Bias. Neutral.

Type. [+]

Body. Key policies of EU27 will be adopted by the UK just as these
are nowadays adopted by EEA members.

Condition. UK leaves the EU.

Promisee. C.

Assessment. Pending.

4. EU27 may constitute a better approximation to an optimum size and
structure than EU28. EU (EU27 as well as EU28) is a complex body
of entities, which profits from, (i) interior globalisation and economy of
scale, (ii) simplified internal decision making (e.g. having fewer, or less
influential members), and (iii) maximising the impact of its policy choices
and internal regulation.

In an optimal configuration those countries which only follow a subset
of the EU internal agreements and regulations are preferably outside the
EU. However, non-members must not be a threat to stability. Such non-
members will be termed EU followers. Norway is the paradigmatic example of an EU follower. Followers outside the EU increase the impact
of EU decision making, while not contributing to the complexity of it.

Moving the UK from member status to follower status could only take
place if the UK withdrew on its own initiative. Is it likely that the UK will
end up in a follower role with respect to EU27? Not all EU28 members
agree on this matter. There are arguments for why the UK withdrawal
may work out positively for EU27:

(a) The UK has negotiated a very strong position involving a combination of special arrangements not shared by other members. In
hindsight, perhaps too many concessions have been made to the UK
by other EU member states. After the UK has left the EU, the EU
will be more homogeneous.

(b) The population of the UK will not accept a much lower standard of
living compared with other surrounding EU27 member states. Thus,
assuming that acting as an EU follower is a condition for prosperity

(which seems to be the assumption for existing EU followers), it is plausible that the UK will act as an EU follower in due time.

(c) UK can be forced into accepting lower average wages so that it will offer some services more cheaply than any EU27 member would do on the long run.

(d) Even in combination with the EU followers mentioned above, the UK is unlikely to constitute a block which is a challenge to EU27.

Of course this argument may divide EU27 if some countries expect lose UK support within the EU for important positions they favour.

5. EU27 features a better political equilibrium than EU. In particular, the role of France, as the state which leads in large scale technology and which is now and in the foreseeable future the only nuclear power within EU27, becomes obviously stronger than it was in EU28. EU27 will profit from the stronger role of France (in comparison with France's role in the current EU).

6. EU27 may well adopt and come to share some of the values sought by the UK, and may improve its operation by so doing.

   - Could the EU have become too large in the following sense: that further unification must come at the cost of a loss of diversity, a loss which outweighs for some member states the gains (for the entire EU) that come with more uniformity.

   - One may speculate that it is a weakness of the EU that the issue of preservation of policy diversity within the EU has been insufficiently addressed. Conceivably Brexit triggers a future development of EU27 so that no other member states will find now or in a foreseeable future similarly significant incentives for leaving the EU straightjacket than the UK now claims to find.

7. Sometimes Brexit is compared with the divorce of a long standing marriage, i.e. that it is bound to be a painful process. This comparison is flawed because EU (EU27) membership does not come with the promise not to leave. One could imagine, idealistically, a future where entering, leaving, and subsequent re-entering the EU was done on a regular basis.[1]

---

[1] For the Eurozone it is considered a problem by some authors that moving out, if only on a temporary basis, is not facilitated by the Maastricht Treaty.

But taking the divorce comparison seriously, it may be concluded that a divorce can very well be a success for all parties involved, it depends very much on how the divorce is put into effect. For child custody, the UK and EU27/28 have joint activities and programs the future of which needs to be safeguarded somehow (ESA, Euratom, Erasmus Program, to mention some).

8. EU28 may have been in need of a new collective enemy since the end of the cold war. Although Russians play that role with glamour, Russian activity is insufficient as an outside treat and. Having a permanent focus on the Russian capture of the Crimea is not so plausible assuming that EU27 has little to gain from close ties with the Russian speaking population of Ukraine. Now the UK has offered itself as a political and economic competitor on a gold plate which contributes to unification within EU27/28.

   Some positive side effects of the forthcoming UK-EU27 rivalry are already visible for EU27/28. In particular the need for an effective French-German cooperation, which lies at the basis of the EU, and which is still a necessary condition for its success, has become acutely felt.

9. Improved chances for taking back financial control (by EU27) from 'The City'.

10. Improved chances for taking back control (by EU27) over the automotive industry.

11. Improved chances for taking back academic control by EU27 institutions, while Oxford and Cambridge will be less able to profit from UK's EU membership.

12. For direct neighbours of the UK within EU27: it is an advantage to serve as a gateway for the EU27 to the outside world.

13. For the 19 Eurozone members within EU27: the position of the Euro within the EU27 becomes stronger, than it is in EU28, as a consequence of the Pound Sterling (GBP) moving out.

The following arguments might be put forward in spite of not being amenable to quantification.

- Outperforming the UK in economic terms is a fundamental challenge for EU27 neighbours of the UK. If that can be done, the strength of the EU, as well as the advantage of EU membership has been proven beyond reasonable doubt.

- From an EU27 perspective it is hard to understand exactly which step forward the UK intends to achieve by putting Brexit into effect. Assuming that EU membership is a profitable state for all of its members and that the UK loses the significant prerogatives[2] which it has accumulated for itself during the last 40 years, it is hard to see how Brexit can be a success, even in principle, for the UK. The EU can change its structure but some patience is required. Why the UK cannot show this form of patience is hard to understand from an EU27/28 perspective.

- The UK leaving the EU creates an increased probability that internal stress within the UK brings fragmentation about with Irish unification and Scottish EU membership as conceivable consequences on the long term. Such events might reconstruct EU27 into an EU27 with England outside and Scotland inside the EU.

- If the result of leaving the EU proves disappointing from a UK perspective a subsequent policy change may take place in the UK and re-entry into the EU may be sought. Upon re-entry, when asked for, the UK would need to adopt the Euro. This very scenario seems to be a rather unique scenario which ends up in a stage where the UK actually enters not only the EU but the Eurozone as well.

- The remarkable collection of lies which have been produced, almost unchallenged and on a systematic basis, by leading UK politicians, before and after Brexit vote and Article 50 triggering suggest that not much is lost in psychological terms for EU27/28 if the UK moves out of the EU.

The mechanisms just listed are rather varied. They range from profiting from a weakened position of the UK after Brexit, exploiting the absence of UK political influence, to planning further development for which UK membership of the EU might constitute a potential stumbling block.

Turning Brexit into a success for both the UK and the remaining EU is an intriguing challenge. By systematically denying the virtues of the EU, however, the proponents of Brexit may turn that challenge into a paradox, as only by

---

[2] The existence of such prerogatives is central in the arguments put forward by Capriglione 2016 [4], who suggests that the EU has made a serious attempt to accommodate UK preferences though to no avail.

valuing some EU properties that the UK prefers to avoid, might it become conceivable that a real and mutually acknowledged advantage could emerge from Brexit, for both sides of the channel.

6.2 Brexit as the best of two worlds from an EU27 perspective

It could be quite difficult to appreciate Brexit as a step forward, from an EU27 perspective, the divorce analogy being particularly unhelpful. Nevertheless, doing so is a useful exercise if only in order to preserve momentum. Here are some possible positions:

- If Brexit leads to a state where the UK outperforms the EU27 (in a way not now expected from the EU side) then this proves that the EU can and must be reformed, for instance by becoming more 'democratic', less protectionist, less amenable to clientism, and more insisting on compliance with its own regulations.

  If, on the contrary, the UK performs poorly outside the EU, the viability of the EU design and operation acquires a unique confirmation.

- The one size fits all perception of European unification is potentially problematic. Brexit brings that message home in a way the EU can't miss. Taking a variety of preferences into account while profiting from an economy of scale will require the EU to be more flexible than it has been towards the UK.

- Brexit was a vote for change powered by older voters, most of whom have for the largest part of their life experienced the UK as an EU member state, with young voters in a conservative role. After Brexit the political scene in Europe is more complex than before, and also more complex than it would have been with Remain. Novel structures and patterns will emerge, new forms of competition will be developed and tested. Why not give Brexit the benefit of doubt as a manifestation of creative destruction.

- As a piece of political theater Brexit is highly intriguing, and perhaps, some years form now Brexit will be viewed as having been an effective step towards a necessary redesign of the EU as enshrined in the Lisbon Treaty. Portraying Brexit as the UK stepping down from a responsibility to work towards a stronger position of Europe in the world at large is implausible and unconvincing. Brexit need not be understood as 'an erroneous political decision' as in Capriglione 2016 [4].

6.3 Making Brexit a success for UK+EU27

Whatever the path leading to a Brexit deliverance, the situation thereafter may be understood independently of that path. Even if many mistakes were made during the process, the outcome may conceivably be preferable to Remain for both UK and EU27/28. With UK+EU27 we will denote the cooperating combination of UK and EU27 after the UK has left the EU. The best arguments in favour of Brexit are arguments that work at the UK+EU27 level. Here are arguments of that form.

6.3.1 Balancing East and West

Suppose one believes that Russia is worried about an ever increasing EU to the West of it. Brexit reduces that worry and for that reason simplifies the process of incorporating Ukraine into EU on the long run. If EU27 must choose between EU27+UK and EU27+Ukraine the choice is not easy but it is plausible to take EU27+Ukraine for the stronger option on the long run.

If one believes this mechanism then it is even preferable from an EU27 perspective (heading towards EU27+Ukraine) that the UK after Brexit acquires strong connections with Russia.

6.3.2 Options for UK+EU27 presence and impact

In principle, Brexit is an advantage for both EU27 and UK if the combination UK+EU27 is functioning so much better than EU28 would have been working that this difference creates added value for all 28 states involved. This is a counterfactual matter because one compares scenario's which cannot both take place. With HEU28 we denote the hypothetical EU consisting of EU28 after the UK has left the EU. It is assumed that at least for some years (say during a period of 10 years after Brexit takes effect) an assessment of the (hypothetical) economic performance P(EU28) of HEU28 is possible. This performance can be projected on the UK: P(HEU28/UK) and on EU27: P(HEU28/EU27), so that HEU28 is decomposed as P(HEU28) = P(HEU28/UK)+P(HEU28/EU27).

Label: UK+EU27 outperforms HEU28.

Promiser. $X_{leave}^{EU27/28}$.

Bias. Neutral.

Type. [+]

Body. The combination UK+EU27 will demonstrate effective cooperation
in the international political arena: more specifically P(HEU28/UK)<P(UK)
and P(HEU28/EU27)<P(EU27).

Condition. UK leaves the EU.

Promisee. C.

Assessment. Pending.

Pisani-Ferry et. al. [20] coin the name 'Continental Partnership' for their model of a fruitful and fairly integrated UK+EU27 cooperation, which, in their view, might eventually work for Ukraine and Turkey as well.

If both the UK and EU27 can profit from Brexit, then this indicates that the EU28 is in a suboptimal equilibrium. Either there is too much integration or there is not enough integration, and diminishing that degree of integration, within EU28, would profit most of its member states.

6.4 Promises in favour of Brexit to EU27/28 citizens

Here is a listing of promises with a pro Leave bias that might be made by an EU27/28 citizen X (say a journalist writing in some medium) to another EU27/28 citizen Y.

1. **Promiser.** X.

   Type. [+].

   Body. EU27 will acquire control over Euro clearing.

   Promisee. Y.

   Scope. EU27/28 citizens.

2. **Promiser.** X.

   Type. [+].

   Body. EU27 will acquire competitive position in the financial industry.

   Promisee. Y.

Scope. EU27/28 citizens.

3. **Promiser.** X.

   Type. [+].

   Body. EU27 will take back academic control from the 2 (to 5) leading academic institutions in the UK.

   Promisee. Y.

   Scope. World.

4. **Promiser.** X.

   Type. [+].

   Body. EU27 will acquire decisive control in the automotive industry.

   Promisee. Y.

   Scope. EU27/28 citizens.

5. **Promiser.** X.

   Type. [+].

   Body. EU27 will acquire control in the financial industry (quite long term development).

   Promisee. Y.

   Scope. EU27/28 citizens.

6. **Promiser.** X.

   Type. [+].

   Body. Eurozone will see new internal dynamics.

   Promisee. Y.

   Scope. EU27/28 citizens.

7. **Promiser.** X

   Type. – (accepting Brexit, a counter promise to the Brexit event promise) promise which is implicit in the Article 50 triggering action).

   Body. EU27/28 prepares for the event of Brexit.

   Promisee. EU27/28-citizens.

   Scope. World.

6.5 Brexit as a plausible step forward for the UK and for the EU27

Is it necessarily the case that, if Brexit is good for the UK, that there is a structural problem with the EU, which needs to be solved in order to prevent further departures of member states? If so then solving the EU problem first, and considering whether or not a subsequent Brexit brings further advantages thereafter, would be the best way to go.

Of all EU28 member states the UK is the most plausible candidate for a state which might (i) be successful outside the EU in the long run, and (ii) be in need of maintaining a very well-defined national identity. Suppose that the UK is, in principle, able to become an extremely competitive economic unit, in the long run, outperforming all EU27 members. Then out of the four freedoms of the EU (freedom of movement of, goods, services, capital, and people) in particular the freedom of movement of people bites. That is, by having to allow arbitrary numbers of EU27 citizens to enter the UK, the UK is indeed at risk of losing its national identity. Accommodating the unlimited freedom of movement for people is just too high a price for simplified access to the markets of EU27 members.

In other words, the EU does not provide a setting in which member states can become successful as nations, it rather provides a setting in which the whole of the EU can effectively compete with other parts of the world. Now it is conceivable, for whatever reason, that only the UK (within EU28) could potentially outperform all other EU27 member states to such an extent that freedom of movement of people would create an unsustainable influx from other EU countries.

One may imagine an 'EEA light' in which a member state traded as if it were an EEA member, but needed not open its borders for the movement of people from EU (EU27). In that scenario, the UK might compensate for disallowing an influx of workers from other EU27 states by paying an additional annual fee to the EU budget; this could be done in such a manner that the additional fee correlated positively (e.g. proportionally) with the trade surplus that the UK created with EU27, with some correction applied each year for the actual influx of people from EU27. Designing a mechanism for the latter correction is not easy, as there should not be a premium for the UK on admitting (from EU27 members) preferably or even exclusively very talented, or capable, or highly skilled, or merely wealthy persons. Indeed freedom of movement of people is intended to allow jobless persons to look for better opportunities, in other members of the EU, and not merely produce a level playing field for trade; otherwise, a very competitive branch of industry (say within the UK) could destroy similar branches of industry elsewhere (in EU27), thereby creating unemployment which could be resolved, even in part, by worker mobility. Trying to find this sort of arrangement, the UK should not be portrayed as being despicable or indulging in cherry picking from the EU menu.

Summing up, even if moving towards a USE27 (United States of Europe with 27 members) constitutes the best option for EU27, it may be the case that UK+USE27 has more potential than EU28 along with a slower evolution towards a USE28. The principal question remains, why has the EU not been designed as a coalition of competing members states, each of which are striving for world-wide prominence? And given the apparent conclusion that the EU has been designed with more integration than necessary for providing a level playing field to competing economies, is it not simply a feature of the design of the EU that the UK alone is preferable outside, while a corresponding preference does not apply to any other of the EU28 members?

Restructuring the EU in such a manner that each member state M could opt out of the freedom of movement principle, by way of financial compensation to another member state N (which does allow freedom of movement from all other members), might create a version of the EU that faithfully issues the following promise, currently not promised by the current form of the EU:

Promiser. EU28 Council and Commission.

Bias. Pro Remain (for all member states including the UK).

Type. [+].

Body. EU membership produces for each of its members an optimal context for the social, cultural, and economic development of the nation.

Condition. Each member state is given a flexible and dynamic choice on tolerance for influx of people from other member states, in such a manner that relatively low tolerance (or relatively selective tolerance) for influx of people may be compensated by a relatively high contribution to the EU budget.

Promisee. EU28 member states.

Scope. EU citizens.

Were EU28 to be able to issue this promise, Brexit would not be of much use to the UK. The whole idea of freedom of movement, as a principled requirement for profiting from the EU, is problematic. Granted that the EU came about as a mechanism for preventing continental conflict, resolved by brute force, it is not at all clear why that mechanism must or even can be developed in such a direction that the very definition of national objectives becomes problematic.

Finally, one could also posit a moral argument for allowing the UK a flexible arrangement on freedom of movement, within the EU. The issue of managing that freedom may be independent of the UK, but it becomes more pronounced in the case of the UK, say, compared to the cases of Norway or Switzerland. Having played a twofold role, at great cost, in resolving a world war that came about from the continent, has the UK not earned the right to ask for a more optimal context in which to promote its national interests? What gives the EU the right to demand of its members abdication from so much of their national identities? And, how can the EU be so intransigently blind to the fact that the two countries for which freedom of movement of people constitutes a problem (UK and Switzerland) are also countries which have not caused any regional armed conflict in the last 150 years. With what justification can the intention to preserve a national identity within the EU, by limiting the influx of people from other member states, be stigmatized as cherry picking?

7

Promises and the general election of Thursday June 8 2017

The general election in June 2017 provides an opportunity for additional appreciation of the role of promises in connection with Brexit. In this chapter, we will consider the occurrence of promises in party manifestos, as well as the evolution of promise bias for promises made in relation to Brexit through the election phase. We will also comment on the side effects of unpredicted events and disasters on said evolution.

7.1 Party manifestos as a bundle of promises

In advance of a general election, a UK political party produces a manifesto. A manifesto typically contains an analysis of the state of the UK, and a package of promises, in the form of new policies. To juxtapose opposition positions, such promises can also be assessed as threats, by putting emphasis on negative consequences or by various forms of framing. For example, framing a Conservative government promise on how to go about asking elderly people to pay for care, while still living in their own home, has been successfully branded by Labour politicians as a so-called 'dementia tax', thus turning a promise into a threat.

The framing of promises in a party manifesto, and the very conception that such promises are binding, are connected with the expectation that there will be a single party majority government. Thus promises play a fundamental role in general elections in the UK. The manifesto of a party contains a survey of promises, which the party intends to promote, and which in particular the party intends to keep, and will be expected to keep, implicitly conditional on being able to constitute a government on the basis of the election outcome.

Now, in the UK system, the House of Lords is not formally bound to follow such promises, once the government proceeds with its attempts to put them in practice. The Salisbury Doctrine (see e.g. Dymond & Deadman 2006 [7]), however, comprises a promise made by the House of Lords not to obstruct a proposal agreed to by the House of Commons indefinitely, provided said proposal may be understood to reflect the will of the people. A sufficient criterion for this is that it was as an intention included in the election manifesto of the governing party (which 'by definition' has thus obtained a workable majority during the most recent elections).

7.1.1 A rationale for hard Brexit compatible promises in the Conservative manifesto

The slogan 'better no deal than a bad deal'[1] as it went with the Conservative election campaign may potentially play a role in the final stage of the Brexit process as follows. Once the outcome of Brexit negotiations with EU27/28 is available it may involve a so-called hard Brexit. Assuming the House of Commons accepts this outcome, the next phase is that the House of Lords must accept it as well, even if a majority of its members is known to think otherwise and even if a majority of its members would expect a second referendum about the modalities of terminating EU membership to turn down the prospect of a hard Brexit.

Political maneuvering is subtle. Convincing parliament of the success of a desirable outcome in the forthcoming Brexit negotiations, whatever that may be, seems to be important to PM Theresa May, because only in the presence of that certainty can negotiations be performed in the most effective manner. On the other hand, to make the House of Lords swallow a hard Brexit, perhaps in third reading, an appeal to the Salisbury Doctrine seems to have become the preferred mechanism. This requires that the government base its proposals on a manifesto, which contains the desired outcome as one of its promises. So, what the Conservative government needed was a new and updated manifesto rather than a larger majority, but installing a new manifesto required it to have a general election as well. With 330 seats, the Conservative party had a majority, as used by David Cameron in the role of PM. That majority, however, could not remotely be claimed to be based on a manifesto that covered a hard Brexit, as

---

[1] See p. 36 of the 2017 Conservative Manifesto, `https://www.conservatives.com/manifesto`.

a potential Conservative policy objective, which is a necessity for applying the Salisbury Doctrine.

In order to safeguard the application the Salisbury Doctrine, when debating the outcome of the forthcoming Brexit negotiations, an electoral majority, supporting a decisive government, with clear manifestos (mentioning 'no deal' or some comparable form of hard Brexit) as an acceptable outcome, would suit the PM. Indeed unless it could be guaranteed, in advance, that the House of Lords would have no other option than to follow the House of Commons on the matter, taking a firm stand during the Brexit negotiations would be unconvincing. For this argument, the size of majority which the post election government can bring together is of lesser importance; what matters is that the government can keep that promise at all, and in a predictable manner. Here, we observe the ineffectiveness of assuming obligation, and the more fragile reality of promises.

New elections could provide the Conservative government with a new rendering of 'The Will Of The People'. However, Labour was unwilling to enter the 2017 campaign on the same premise as the Conservative Party, that these elections were held primarily to secure Conservative Party guarantees (via the Salisbury Doctrine) for a Conservative Government in its dealing with the House of Lords. Instead Labour directed its campaign in a far more social direction, thus leaving the Conservatives exposed to some unfortunate consequences of their long standing austerity approach to the economic challenges of the UK. The election of June 8 2017 failed to strengthen the Conservative majority; indeed, the majority was in fact lost in the process.

Having obtained 318 seats out of 650, it is hard to see that decisive support for a hard Brexit was obtained, and adding 10 DUP seats in order to obtain a majority did not promote the case for a hard Brexit either (see Paragraph 7.5 below for a precise calculation). In the Labour manifesto, no support for either no-deal or for a hard Brexit, in whatever form, can be found, while acceptance of a hard Brexit was somehow implicit in the Labour talk on Brexit outside the manifesto.[2] Therefore support for Labour in the 2017 elections cannot be construed as a manifesto based support for a hard Brexit.

---

[2] See Chapter 'Negotiating Brexit' in the 2017 Labour manifesto `http://www.labour.org.uk/index.php/manifesto2017/brexit`. Leaving the single market is mentioned as a plausible option in the Labour manifesto, though with need of compensation in terms of an additional trade agreement, but an exit from the single market is not portrayed as a necessity.

7.1.2 The Salisbury Doctrine as a generic conditional promise

Let p be a promise contained in the manifesto M_P of party P. Let I_p be a proposal which the intention of which to implement p. The Salisbury doctrine may be understood as a mechanism which generates for each member X of the House of Lords the following promise which can be used by the government when needed.

Promiser. X.

Type. +.

Body. To support, or at least not to prevent, that ultimately in a third reading I_p is agreed to, and that only moderate adaptations are required.

Conditions.
- the promise p occurs in M_P,
- P has obtained a majority in the Commons,
- I_p has been proposed by the government and has been accepted by a Commons majority, and
- The government indicates that the case calls for an application of the Salisbury Doctrine.

Promisee. UK Gov.

Scope. UK citizens.

7.2 Some follow-up promises

Immediately after the UK general election the following promises made it into the media:

1. The Conservative government will carry on with the same PM (Theresa May).

2. Brexit negotiations will commence on June 19 as planned.

3. the new government will have the support of the DUP.

4. Brexit will occur as planned and the effectuation of Article 50 is not in doubt.

5. If the UK Brexit negotiators prove unwilling to adopt the EU27/28 prepared agenda for these negotiations including a firm scheduling of topics to be discussed the EU may need a full year to develop a renewed negotiation mandate for their negotiators from EU27/28

7.3 Promise termination and simplification

In the context of Brexit, a promise, say P may come to the end of its life-cycle in many different ways. Here is a survey of ways in which that may work.

Promiser withdrawal. If the promiser is a candidate who has lost in their constituency then the promise has evaporated by the promiser being made incapable of contributing to the keeping of the promise. Promises made by candidates are live only as long as candidates are politically active. There need not be a penalty for the promiser, in terms of degradation of trust; this matters because they might be candidates in a forthcoming election as well.

Condition invalidated locally. If the promiser is a candidate who has lost in their constituency (electoral district), and the promise was conditional on their winning the seat, then the promise evaporates by virtue of the condition becoming false. There need not be a penalty for the promiser, in terms of degradation of trust; which, again matters because they might be a candidate in a forthcoming election as well.

Condition invalidated globally. If the promiser is a candidate who has won in their constituency (electoral district), and the promise was conditional on their party acquiring a majority in the House of Commons, and the latter was not achieved then the promise terminates by the condition becoming false. Again there need not be a penalty for the promiser in terms of degradation of trust, which matters because they might be candidate in a forthcoming election as well.

Promise withdrawal. If the promiser concludes, from the election outcome, that the promise is unlikely to be kept (e.g. the promise to accept a no deal outcome of Brexit negotiations), the the promiser may withdraw the promise, which may (but need not) come with a penalty on trust from the public.

Promise simplification by condition removal. A promiser may actually reinforce a promise by repeating it, in a simplified way, i.e. without the conditions that have become true as an effect of the election result. Promise simplification comes with a potential gain of trust for the promiser who has shown that the conditional promise has proven sustainable in the face of the election just held.

Steady promise kept. This case is best explained via an example: the promise made by Theresa May to keep working towards a successful Brexit was kept also after the disappointing outcome of the general election. As it stands this promise is kept and at the same time it stands out as it involves a continuous commitment (i.e. it is a steady promise) which may expire only after the UK has left the EU, and this step has either become a success or has opened a path towards success.

Steady promise not kept. A steady promise (e.g. to strive for hard Brexit) may terminate by not being kept. Termination of a steady promise by not keeping it come with loss of trust for the promiser. A promise which is not kept may or may not be withdrawn. Withdrawing a promise may be done in order to minimise the expected loss of trust.

Promise not kept. We have no example of a promise which was terminated because it turned out not to be kept in the first week after the general election of June 2017.

Promise kept. We have no example of a promise which was terminated because it turned out to be kept in the first week after the general election of June 2017.

7.4 Updating expectations in connection with Brexit

The following changes in expectations can be formulated as a consequence of the election result, assuming a pre-election view on expectations based on the expectation that the result would be a stronger Conservative majority. Changes of expectations can all be phrased in terms of an increment. The following expectations have increased, however minimally. These changes, i.e. the sign given, seem to be plausible for all agents involved.

1. Brexit will not take place.

2. The Brexit negotiation period will be extended.

3. There will be a second referendum on EU membership.

4. Scotland will stay within the UK.

5. The UK will join EFTA.

6. The UK will remain within the EEA (though not as a consequence of EU membership).

7. The UK will avoid a hard Brexit (crash out to WTO rules of trade without a special agreement with EU27/28).

8. The Pound will drop below parity with the Euro during 2017. (This might just happen in an extended period of political uncertainty.)

9. The housing market in London will crash during 2017.

10. The UK will enter a period of recession beginning in 2017.

11. Interest rates within the UK will be increased during 2017.

12. The UK budget deficit will grow over expectation (in relation to the last budget) in 2017 and 2018.

13. Proponents of a hard Brexit among the Conservative MPs have a dominant position.

14. If (new) general elections are held before the end of 2019 Labour will be victorious and may well obtain a workable majority.

15. The management of the Labour party is strong and stable.

For some events the change in expectation is quite hard to assess. The case can be made that the expectation for the following events has decreased as a consequence of the election result.

1. There will be a change of PM within 2 years. Indeed, for C&UP (Conservative and Unionist Party, Conservatives for short) it is a significant risk to have a leadership crisis which may result in new elections.

2. There will be yet another general election before the new Parliament has ended. For the C&UP new elections create a risk of losing power which they won't easily take.

3. The outcome of the Brexit negotiations is rejected in either House. Indeed the plausibility for looking for some form of soft Brexit has increased so much that it has become more likely that Brexit negotiations produce an agreement with multi-party support.

Taking all these changes of estimation together, and assuming that Theresa May in fact preferred and continues to prefer a softer Brexit over a hard Brexit it may be concluded that by (i) calling for new elections, and (ii) campaigning so poorly that Labour could do over expectation, and (iii) ending up in a state where Labour could do even better at the peril of C&UP, though (iv) in a state which admits precisely one scenario (a pragmatic cooperation with DUP) for remaining in power, the position of Theresa May has been strengthened rather than improved, though in a paradoxical manner. The risk that removing her from Downing Street 10 poses to conservative MPs, whose seats may in some cases be hard to defend when yet another general election is needed, has clearly increased.

Of course these remarks are time-stamped just after the election, and for that reason don't take any subsequent events into account. Quantified estimation of the subjective probability of potential future events is by necessity time dependent. What can be asserted, however, is that say one week after the general election the PM may well have strengthened rather than weakened her position.

7.5 Promises in the aftermath of the general election

Promises made by politicians with the entire public in scope are less useful in the aftermath of the election and referendum. Rather than complicating the scene with additional promises that may be difficult to keep simplifying the situation by doing away with existing promises is a practical way to proceed. Immediately after the election these mechanisms play a role.

While the production and broadcasting of promises has played a central role in the up and until referendum and general election there seems to be less to gain from working with promises in this stage. However an agreement between the C&UP and DUP which may be forthcoming, has been announced by way of a promise.

Promiser. Theresa May.

Bias. Pro Tory Remain (in power).

Type. +

Body. I will lead a C&UP government with support of DUP.

Promisee. UK Parliament.

Scope. UK citizens.

The numerical motivation for this arrangement may be expressed as a promise:

> **Promiser.** Theresa May.
>
> **Bias.** Pro Tory Remain (in power).
>
> **Type.** +
>
> **Body.** A C&UP government with support of DUP will command a majority of 6 votes.
>
> **Promisee.** UK Parliament.
>
> **Scope.** UK citizens.

Calculating an estimation of an expected majority can be done as follows: (i) he number of voting MPs is found by subtracting from the totality of MPs the absentees and the 4 non-voting functionaries (2 conservatives and 2 from Labour): Voting MPs = 650 MPs − 7 MPs (Sinn Fein absentees) − 1 MP (speaker) − 3 MPs (Deputy Speakers) = 639 MPs, (ii) therefore so that 320 MPs are needed for a majority vote (assuming all opposition MPs vote homogeneously as well); (iii) now the C&UP has 316 voting MPs (not counting the speaker and the First Deputy Chairman of Ways and Means) and the DUP is represented with 10 MPs (all voting), which in total makes 326 MPs, that is 6 more than the 320 MPs needed for a majority vote in the 'worst case scenario'.

Stated differently, with all voting MPs present and voting according to the various party lines, the forthcoming Queen's Speech would be accepted with 326-313 votes, a sizeable difference of 13 votes.

According to various newspapers the following promise was issued in order to acquire support from Conservative MPs.

> **Promiser.** Theresa May.
>
> **Bias.** Pro Tory Remain (in power).
>
> **Type.** +
>
> **Body.** I will listen to all views on Brexit from Conservative MP's.
>
> **Promisee.** Committee of Conservative MPs (backbench).
>
> **Scope.** Conservative MPs.

Promises may well play a significant role in the post-election phase too but such promises constitute steps within the professional political group rather than being meant for an audience at large. Moreover promises with the entire public in scope will be documented intentions rather than documented expectations.

Promiser. Leader of Scottish Conservatives.

Bias. Pro Tory Remain (in power).

Type. +

Body. Brexit will be designed with input from a wider group of MPs than a mere Conservative government.

Promisee. Conservative and DUP MPs.

Scope. UK public.

Voices against a C&UP plus DUP joint venture can be phrased as promises: e.g.

Promiser. John Major (former conservative PM).

Bias. Pro Tory Remain (in power).

Type. [+]

Body. Making the new government explicitly dependant on DUP risks creating significant problems in Northern Ireland. It is not necessary for installing a new government either.

Promisee. Conservative MPs.

Scope. UK public.

The forthcoming Brexit negotiations create a stream of promises as well:

Promiser. Theresa May.

Bias. Pro Tory Remain (in power).

Type. +

Body. Brexit will commence on June 19 as it was planned already before the general election.

Promisee. Conservative MPs.

Scope. UK public.

In spite of the fact that the general election result seems to have removed, at least in theory, the option to make use of the Salisbury Doctrine for pushing through a hard Brexit the following promise stands out so it seems.

Promiser. David Davis.

Bias. Pro Tory Remain (in power).

Type. +

Body. No deal is a feasible outcome of the forthcoming Brexit negotiations.

Promisee. Conservative MPs.

Scope. UK public.

7.6 Events: the Grenfell Tower fire

On June 14 2017 the Grenfell Tower, a high rise tower block for public housing located in the Royal Borough of Kensington and Chelsea, was entirely destroyed by a catastrophic fire with deadly consequences for many people.[3]

Harold MacMillan, a former conservative MP, claimed that this event, and its unfolding, constituted a major threat for any government. The Grenfell Tower fire focused attention on a number of issues that had been invisible during the election campaign: implications of austerity, implications of deregulation, implications and effectiveness of EU regulations, quality of work of a number of high ranking conservative politicians, implications of the gap between social classes in London, the quality taking lessons of previous fires into account. The catastrophic fire has immediately led to the expression of claims, requests and promises from various sides, as well as to complaints about the promises being insufficient, and so on.

Unavoidably these issues are becoming connected with the non-Brexit related issues at stake in the recent elections, manifestly highlighting Labour claims regarding the need to strengthen the structure and functioning of the welfare state.

The key conditional promise of the general election, that upon a victorious result the UK would be led by a strong and stable government, was turned around into the claim that the UK government did not handle the Grenfell Tower fire sufficiently well: no victory, no strong and stable government, no room for promising that a strong and stable government would be successful with forthcoming Brexit negotiations either.

---

[3] For further information see `https://en.wikipedia.org/wiki/Grenfell_Tower_fire`.

7.7 What would replace promises in election-free episodes?

In the absence of elections, promises might seem to be less prominent. In place of promises, a veil of non-intentional claims include 'news' and 'fake news', etc, may be offered as evidence of success without intent. Very detailed information about the economic development in key sectors, e.g. about the the health of the NHS, and the strength, readiness and effectiveness of the police system, may take the place of promises for years to come. This downplaying of promises is now seen in the USA, where there is a complete disconnection between what was promised and observable outcomes.

With promises becoming less prominent impositions gain prominence, for instance:

Imposer. Keir Starmer (shadow Brexit negotiator).

Bias. Pro soft Brexit.

Type. [+]

Body. Theresa may must now acknowledge that no-deal is not an option and that hard is an undesirable outcome of the Brexit negotiations.

Imposee. Theresa May.

Scope. UK public.

8

Brexit as a conceptual issue

The most unequivocal assertion concerning Brexit has been the statement that 'Brexit is Brexit' (B=B). In its superficial triviality, this assertion indicates that Brexit, whatever it is, is a real phenomenon waiting to happen, once it takes place one will know whether or not the real Brexit has come.

By asserting B=B it is also claimed, or at least reaffirmed, that the referendum had substance, and, at the same time, the referendum outcome was transmuted into a necessity, obliging the government to act accordingly. The slogan eviscerated degrees of freedom to such an extent that a virtually deterministic path of action towards triggering Article 50 lay ahead.

It was argued in paragraph 2.6 above that these steps, taken by Theresa May, only appear to promote the Brexiter's case, whereas in fact the Brexiters might better have fiercely protested against making more out of the referendum outcome than needed.

In terms of content B=B means that (i) the EU as it stands, including its likely trajectory in the years ahead, is not an attractive locus for the UK, and that leaving the EU now is the better option for the UK; (ii) moving the UK out of the EU is going to be done as soon as reasonably possible. Although this interpretation of Brexit seems clear, it gives rise to many questions, which surface when one contemplates potential states of affairs, after the UK has left the EU. A survey of parameters for this 'state space' of options may be helpful. Taken together, a combinatoric explosion of conceivable futures, without any apparent grand design, emerges.

8.1 Hard Brexit versus soft Brexit

After the Brexit has been completed, including a possible transitional phase as suggested by some politicians, the UK may find itself in any of the following states:

- Inside or outside the EU.

- With or without an adequate divorce agreement. The divorce agreement must cover: (i) rights and duties of UK citizens in EU27 and rights of EU27 citizens inside the UK, (ii) an exit fee (if any), (iii) a policy for dealing with the Irish border, and (iv) minimal arrangements for cooperation on security matters.

- Outside the EU, though with an EU modified in such a manner that there is a special status for Scotland and for Northern Ireland which then both remain inside the EU as well as inside the UK.

- Inside or outside the jurisdiction of the CJEU.

- Partially inside the jurisdiction of the CJEU.

- Inside the jurisdiction of the CJEU but with modified rules of operation of ECOJ, turning it into some form of joint venture between the UK and EU27.

- Inside or outside the European single market (ESM), (the so-called passporting mechanism including 9 different passports for the financial sector are an ESM feature[1]).

- Outside the single market but within a single financial market which keeps the passporting rights of UK institutions in place while not committing the UK to the freedom of movement of persons.

- Inside the single market though with one or more novel opt outs in connection the freedom of movement of people (the only controversial freedom among the so-called four freedoms on which the single market is based).

---

[1] For details on passporting see BBA Brexit Quick Brief #3: `https://www.bba.org.uk/wp-content/uploads/2016/12/webversion-BQB-3-1.pdf` (accessed June 19, 2017).

- Inside or outside the European customs union (ECU).

- Inside the customs union though with novel rights for the UK to engage in bilateral trade treaties of certain forms with selected other parts of the world (for instance with commonwealth countries).

- Inside or outside Schengen agreement.

- Inside or outside the Euro area.[2]

- Inside or outside EEA.

- Inside or outside EFTA.

- Outside EEA and EFTA but with arrangements similar to EEA arrangements (Norway option).

- Outside EFTA but with arrangements similar to Switzerland arrangements (Swiss option).

- Inside or outside the ECHR.

- Outside EEA, EFTA, ESM, ECU and with novel agreements comparable to the Swiss option but more based on equal terms.

- With new agreements with WTO on agriculture.

- With new roles in one or more of the EU decentralised agencies.

- With new roles in one or more EU institutions (e.g. EIB, ECA, EDPS, CERT).

- With new arrangements on policing, security, and/or military investment and operations,

- With new agreements on ESA, Euratom, CERN, Science and Research funding, Erasmus Program, etc.,

- With adapted trade agreements with Canada, Ukraine, Turkey, EFTA countries, etc.

---

[2] The UK adopting the Euro might be taken for the complete failure of the Brexit agenda, unless it has come with a UK supported restructuring of the principles of the Euro.

Now B=B loses its meaning, if one is open ended towards the possible outcomes of the process, and in particular, if one intends to preserve the *status quo ante* as much as possible. Which of these (combinations of) options constitutes a soft Brexit, and which ones constitute a hard Brexit, is far from clear. Below the following definition is used:

Defiinition 8.1.1 *A hard Brexit is a Brexit which is based on an adequate divorce agreement and which leaves the UK outside EU, CJEU, ESM, ECU, and EEA, and the agreement for which contains only marginal provisions for compensating for the effects of these changes.*

Defiinition 8.1.2 *A moderately hard Brexit is a Brexit which is based on an adequate divorce agreement and which leaves the UK inside the ECU and outside EU, CJEU, ESM, and EEA, and is arranged in such a manner that the agreement about it contains only marginal provisions for compensating for the effects of these changes.*

In advance of the announcement of the general election, a hard Brexit outcome was (generally accepted as constituting) an acceptable outcome of a Brexit negotiation, implementing the will of the people (though not in a manner that would provably pass the House of Lords). Thus, the following assertion was valid true after Article 50 had been triggered and at least until the announcement of the general election of June 8, 2019.

Proposition 8.1.1 *'Better a hard Brexit than no Brexit.'*

Remarkably the UK chancellor, Philip Hammond, stated just in advance of the Brexit negotiations that a hard Brexit would be a very bad outcome. The chancellor's statement concurs with voices from Brexit opponents and from various industrial factions. This leaves open the question of whether he supports Proposition 8.1.1, and if not, what (according to him) the outcome of the EU referendum could have possibly meant otherwise.

For instance it could have meant that the UK being outside the EU is a preferable state of affairs (according to the will of the people) but not to be reached against arbitrarily high costs. It is intriguing that the government interpretation of an advisory referendum can produce something stronger than a preference. If the advice given by entity A (here the people) is that action B (here Brexit) must be taken, then what does it mean to follow the advice: to do B or to make a best effort in the direction of B?

The chancellor's statement also leaves open the question if he would consider a moderately hard Brexit bad or even very bad.

Defiinition 8.1.3 *Crashing out is the name for a (conceivably forthcoming) short and unfriendly process leading to a a position like a hard Brexit but without an adequate divorce agreement. Crashing out is an unfriendly divorce.*

Every option closer to the EU, other than crashing out, cannot be arrived at without active support and cooperation of EU27/28. Therefore it follows that, if the will of the people, as it has been revealed by the referendum, is to leave the EU, then crashing out must be acceptable to the people as well. The policy of Theresa May has been based on this reasoning pattern. This argument leads to the following rephrasing of 'better no deal than a bad deal'

Proposition 8.1.2 *Better crashing out towards a hard Brexit than having no Brexit at all.*

The above Proposition merely summarises a logical consequence of a reasonable interpretation of recent events in the UK political system. Portraying members of the UK government, who point to it as a fact of life, as 'bullying the public in the direction of EU27/28', seems out of place. The facts stand, whether one likes them or not. However, the mandate to guide Brexit negotiations on her own terms, which Theresa May claimed to be in need of, was not given to the C&UP on June 9th. This creates an unclear situation: if or when the same government might offer a crash out, as the result of negotiations. Do the Commons follow the will of the people, when accepting a crashed out Brexit, on the authority of Theresa May and her team? And if so, does this imply that they would have to follow suit and accept a crashed out hard Brexit? This problem would have been solved (in the positive direction) in advance had the election result been a clear Conservative majority.

By promising that obtaining a clear conservative majority was an essential asset for Brexit negotiations, in advance of the election, the impression was given that losing such a majority might create problems for these negotiations. The situation is complicated by the fact that, only rarely, a government which commands an absolute majority risks losing that majority at its own initiative. There must have been significant reasons to do so, and this was the argument that was put forward. In Paragraph 7.1.1 above it has been argued that other, equally convincing, arguments for having a general election could be imagined.

Proposition 8.1.3 *By framing Brexit as being primarily about taking back control of the UK borders, and taking back control of long term immigration policies, the theme of Brexit has obtained a focus on an obvious weakness of the structure of the EU. The same objective matters a lot for other countries inside and outside the EU, even if these member states are reluctant to make such worries public.*

By framing Brexit as a issue of immigration control, achieving a moderately hard Brexit can be said to be a success.

Proposition 8.1.4 *A moderately hard Brexit allows the UK to take back control of its borders, while it won't allow the UK freedom of making its own trade agreements with external parties.*

Defiinition 8.1.4 *A soft Brexit takes place if the UK leaves the EU while staying in ECU and ESM. There are many conceivable realisations of a soft Brexit.*

Defiinition 8.1.5 *A medium Brexit takes place if the UK leaves the EU while staying in ECU and in a modified ESM which allows for systematic and flexible immigration control by the UK.*

Proposition 8.1.5 *The bundle of promises made about Brexit in advance of the referendum fails to shed any light on which of the possible outcomes mentioned above have been promised to the UK public to be favoured or disfavoured during Brexit negotiations.*

Proposition 8.1.6 *The general election has produced a (bipartisan) Commons majority which was elected on the basis of two different manifestos both of which indicate that (i) the UK will leave the EU and that, (ii) a hard Brexit is better than no Brexit, though perhaps less undesirable.*

Thus, the general election has produced a setting in which the Commons are less likely to take the outcome of Tory led Brexit negotiations for granted, with the Conservative majority having been lost, while a reasonable reading of the Salisbury Doctrine to a multi-party context binds the Lords to confirmation of an agreement upon its acceptance by the Commons.

8.2 Brexit framing

One of Theresa May's achievements has been to work towards a conceptual framing of Brexit, in which it is primarily about taking back control over the borders of the UK, and, in particular, about the UK having a final say over its immigration policies for the long run. At the same time this framing of Brexit creates conceptual complications: suppose that, after all, in turns out that the limited objectives concerning immigration can be achieved within the EU. Does framing Brexit as an immigration issue imply that Brexit is conditional on a proven impossibility to agree with the EU on immigration? Or, does it imply that a process towards Brexit can be performed, in parallel, with negotiations about intra-EU immigration and emigration, the success of which would interrupt the other process.

On the other hand, suppose one considers the soft Brexit as undesirable, because the UK will thus lose influence within the EU without getting the degrees of freedom it claims to need in return, then the required outcome lies in between a hard Brexit and a soft Brexit. If the moderately hard Brexit is considered economically problematic (for instance because of an expected loss of passporting rights for the City) a Brexit in between a soft Brexit and a moderately hard Brexit needs to be designed; this must involve so-called cherry picking from the side of the EU, which may be impossible.

So-called cherry picking has been ridiculed by several EU27 politicians, which seems to us to be an implausible stand. Recently the German minister of foreign affairs, Gabriel, has suggested that some weakening of a moderately hard Brexit (in our terminology) might be achievable. It seems that from a German point of view, cherry offering is okay, while cherry picking is not—an inconsistent, if not offensive, way of putting things.

It follows, then, that a soft Brexit is not a plausible option either and a paradoxical situation arises. This state of affairs is somehow expressed by the famous and paradoxical slogan 'no deal is better than a bad deal'.

Assuming that the need for the UK to take back control over the influx of people to be the most essential improvement that Brexit is supposed to deliver, the situation is obscured by the fact that precisely the open door policy that, for instance, made so many Poles come to the UK was of a UK making. Notably, Germany avoided that very influx by means of EU compatible policies. The influx of persons from EU27 member states to the EU is now being portrayed falsely as an EU requirement that has already been creating unnecessary problems for the UK.

The mysterious side of the referendum outcome is that it demonstrates an outcry for change, while failing to provide enough intended sense of direction to move toward that change by means of an unambiguous policy. It appears that David Cameron, when proposing the referendum, had not prepared for a policy to be followed after a negative outcome concerning EU membership. It would have been more systematic (at least seen from an outsider's perspective) first to have a new government which was willing to propose a reasonably well-defined Brexit, including a perspective on choices regarding hard versus soft Brexit, and including positions on Euratom, WTO, ESA, CJEU, ECHR, and so on, and then to have a second referendum intended to confirm and to specify in more detail the intention to leave the EU. The second referendum (assuming it confirmed the first one) would produce the natural point of departure for negotiations with the EU.[3]

In both cases, that is without a second referendum, and with a second referendum providing more guidance on how to leave the EU, a true renegotiation of the relations between the UK and EU27/28 would be needed to settle the intended outcome. As discussed earlier, an outcome might be that the UK promises to pay, by way of compensation, for its unwillingness to allow freedom of movement of people. There might be a price that the UK could offer, which makes such a deal attractive for EU27/28. Compensatory cherry picking is not the same as cherry picking, and need not be taken off the table in advance—as if looking for cherries to pick were an unreasonable approach by itself.

By slating the UK's entirely comprehensible and defensible desired choices as 'cherry picking', the EU has deprived itself of the option to use Brexit as a trigger for improving its own internal structure, and for better taking into account the needs of individual member states. This could clearly apply to any issues for which a full understanding arises only after the consequences of various initial policies have become clear (as the world accelerates, and governments are expected to keep pace, this number must surely only increase). Is it reasonable for EU27 leadership to require that past UK governments should have foreseen the need to control the influx of people more than they set out to do? A government incapable of admitting error is also incapable of democracy. That the openness of the UK to an influx of EU citizens has been perceived, by a part of the populace, as having backfired might well have happened to France

---

[3] If one views a referendum as a means to solve a problem inside a governing party then having a second referendum after the general elections and about would preferred ways of Brexiting might be justified at once.

and to Germany just as well (if indeed this is not already clear).

Another attempt for framing Brexit has been to promote jobs and economy as the principal criteria for evaluating a Brexit agreement. Labour MPs, as well as some Conservative MPs, have proposed the latter framing of Brexit. Looking at Brexit in that manner seems to have no basis in past events and promises, and it comprises a simplistic view on the objectives of Brexit. It can be phrased as a proposition, hardly as a promise, and there is no way to connect it to the preceding process.

Proposition 8.2.1 *(Jobs and economy framing of Brexit.) Better a soft Brexit than a hard Brexit which goes at cost of jobs and economic growth.*

Proposition 8.2.2 *(Corbyn after June 9th.) Better a soft Brexit than a no deal (hard) Brexit.*

A major difficulty with this economic framing of Brexit is that such preferences are not expected to enter the parliamentary debate when discussing the outcome of Brexit negotiations.

A remarkable form of framing works as follows. A moderately hard Brexit (leaving the single market) is referred to in positive terms as a Brexit providing access to the single market (ESM), and no more than that. Subsequently a preference is formulated in positive terms only, which amounts to a preference for some form of soft Brexit, though not stated in such terms.

Proposition 8.2.3 *Better inside ESM than to have access to ESM.*

The latter proposition of course has a modified version as follows:

Proposition 8.2.4 *Better inside a UK-tailored ESM than to have access to ESM.*

Here 'UK-tailored' would refer to a reduction of the obligation to allow and facilitate the freedom of movement into the UK for EU27 persons.

8.3 Another milestone: 19 June 2017: start of Brexit negotiations

A key event in the Brexit trajectory was the formal initiation of Brexit negotiations. To what extent does the very fact that negotiations are being held change the state of affairs?

As promised by Theresa May, the Brexit negotiations started on June 19 with David Davis and Michiel Barnier leading both negotiation teams. Newspapers describe the UK position as ill-defined, because it could now be doubted, after the recent general election. Does indeed a so-called hard Brexit in fact have popular support?

After the first day of negotiation Michel Barnier said that:

> The United Kingdom has decided to leave the European Union, it is not the other way around. The United Kingdom is going to leave the European Union, single market and the customs union, not the other way around. So, we each have to assume our responsibility and the consequences of our decisions. And the consequences are substantial.

Although this position has been voiced by David Davis just as well the confirmation by Barnier may be considered to some extent a matter of framing. It moves the UK into a position of having already chosen in favour of a hard Brexit which may not yet be the case. Moreover it creates a setting in which the UK need to perform a humiliating U-turn in order to stay in the ECM after all, thereby mounting pressure on hard Brexit opponents in the UK to mobilise their forces. At the same time, it is compatible with Proposition 8.1 and when firmly adopted it creates preconditions for a Brexit agreement that will not be rejected by the Commons and cannot be rejected by the House of Lords. Of course nothing is given away in either direction as a Brexit deal might contain a reconstruction of major parts of ECU and ESM under different names.

Barnier suggested the notion of a fair deal (probably some form of medium Brexit style hard Brexit), thereby moving the concept no deal to the trash-bin, and leaving the fundamental Tory slogan 'better no deal than a bad deal' in the vacuum thus working against its potential future use in the House of Lords, and portraying crashing out as wrong doing from the side of EU27/28, which he would not want to take responsibility for.

Proposition 8.3.1 *(Barnier) Better a fair deal than no deal.*

Barnier's remarks may be understood as issuing the following promise.

Promiser. Michael Barnier.

Bias. Unknown.

Type. +

Body. A fair deal for a hard Brexit will be obtained in the forthcoming Brexit negotiations.

Condition. An agreement is first reached about a divorce settlement.

Promisee. EU public.

Scope. EU public.

8.4 On the logic of Brexit I: The 'Logic' of Theresa May

From a logical point of view the unfolding of events, after the referendum, is quite non-trivial. Here we will argue that, at least until July 10, 2017, the UK government, and in particular the PM, has chosen a course of action and a sequence of policies which is both comprehensible and systematic.

On the one hand the sequence of steps listed below is consistent with working towards a hard Brexit, but on the other hand the same sequence of actions is also potentially best possible if the hidden agenda of the PM is and has been to avoid Brexit, and in particular to avoid an unconvincing soft Brexit, while taking the low risk of the UK a crashing out towards a hard Brexit.

B=B. Once Brexit had obtained a majority vote in the referendum by stating Brexit = Brexit (B=B), it was unambiguously announced that the UK will leave the EU. The importance of asserting B=B over and over again lies in the implication that Brexit is not a preference over a host of alternatives but that it constitutes a fact of life which will not be scrutinised any further. It is going to happen whether one likes it or not[4].

Speeding towards triggering Article 50. By moving quickly towards the triggering of the EU exit process as specified in Article 50 the internal inconsistency created by viewing the referendum as binding for both possible outcomes in spite of the fact that satisfactory preparations for a negative outcome had not been made, has been fully preserved. As it turns out, a few months later it has become exceedingly difficult for the UK politicians so produce a coherent picture of what they intend to achieve.

Brexit as a bipartisan objective. By having a general election, the fact (expectation, unconditional promise) that the UK will leave the EU has been promoted to the level of inclusion in both manifestos of Conservative and Labour parties. Realisation of Brexit has been taken out of the hands of the Conservatives and a large majority in Parliament has been made responsible for it. Preparations for an application of the Salisbury Doctrine have been made with, remarkably, a bipartisan backing.

---

[4] In computer science jargon: the UK not being a member of the UK was turned into a required post-condition of forthcoming UK policy.

Better no deal than a bad deal. Assuming the exit process, specified in the Lisbon Treaty, there will be negotiations about 'a deal' on Brexit. Viewed from a UK perspective, the outcome of such negotiations may range from good (have the cake and eat it), to bad. By stating that no deal is better than a bad deal it is proclaimed that it is entirely and exclusively up to the UK to leave the EU. Of course the UK cannot guarantee a good deal, as it has no power over EU27/28. But the UK has clarified that the decision to leave the EU is unconditional, it is not a matter of preferences.

It is a misunderstanding to read 'better no deal than a bad deal' as a preference for a hard Brexit. The said preference exclusively follows from the unconditional character (or rather interpretation) of the referendum outcome based Brexit decision.

The responsibility to clarify what no deal means resides as much with EU27/28 as with the UK. Because the TEU (Lisbon Treaty) requires the UK (or any exiting state) to decide first, the EU must be supportive for defining a reasonable exit mechanism. The EU cannot possibly require that an exiting state obtains a good deal, were that the case the EU is merely a prison.

Application of Arrow impossibility. As an case that is primarily about social choice, the Brexit process is sensitive to phenomena related to the *Arrow impossibility theorem* of social choice. This concerns the impossibility of reflecting a logically sound (transitive) set of preferences by means of majority voting, in any circumstances. What this means is that some form of implausibility regarding preferences and revealed preferences potentially cannot be prevented. We provide two examples of how this might work.

Example 1. Let Bremain stand for the UK not leaving the EU. The will of the people may be captured by a preference relation $<_{wop}$. Now it is possible that the will of the people entails the following preferences:

- Bremain $<_{wop}$ Brexit
  (referendum outcome: preference of Brexit over Bremain),

- Soft Brexit $<_{wop}$ Bremain
  (fearing that soft Brexit means giving up influence without sufficient compensation in terms of operational freedom for the UK).

Arrow's impossibility result implies that it may well be true that, at the same time, (refuting transitivity of preferences which suggests Soft Brexit

$<_{wop}$ Brexit):

- Soft Brexit $>_{wop}$ Brexit
  (reluctance to accept the consequences of a hard Brexit; here soft Brexit stands for a Brexit which is guaranteed to be soft by the design of the process leading to it).

Example 2. Focusing on a conceivable no deal hard Brexit the following preferences may potentially be observed.

- Bremain $<_{wop}$ Brexit
  (referendum outcome: preference of Brexit over Bremain),

- No deal hard Brexit $<_{wop}$ Bremain
  (emerging consensus that business must have more of a say and that the people did not vote to get poorer etc.; avoiding a guaranteed no deal hard Brexit),

Arrow's impossibility result now entails that it may well be that at the same time (and refuting transitivity of preferences which suggests No deal hard Brexit $<_{wop}$ Brexit):

- No deal hard Brexit $>_{wop}$ Brexit
  (reacting to perceived EU27/28 arrogance with a rather uncompromising position).

Which, if any, of these examples pertain in the matter at hand: Theresa May's policy is not distracted by any form of this argument. Accepting Brexit as an unconditional fact, the logic of preferences is likely to reveal paradoxes. Such paradoxes come about when complex decisions are made by way of a referendum, which has been done in an irreversible manner, in this case. Theresa May's effective application of Arrow impossibility, in her handling of Brexit, has been not to engage in any form of preferential reasoning, and not to promise any subsequent decision taken by parliament and based on forthcoming new or revealed preferences. The exception, of course, is the following.

A good deal is better than no deal: the intention to have the cake and eat it.
Although this goes without saying, when choosing between the deal that has been found during negotiations and no deal, if the deal is a good deal from a UK perspective then it can be effectively preferred.

In spite of having been ridiculed by several EU27/28 leaders the intention 'to have the cake and eat it' is entirely logical from a UK point of view and reveals no preference that might become controversial or even reversed. By not taking this preference seriously EU27/28 leaders have merely demonstrated an unwillingness to acknowledge politics or for preferential reasoning, in the context of Brexit. This seems to be principally an intent to humiliate the UK.

Not formulating any preference for a soft Brexit. It is only by not formulating any preference for a soft Brexit that all cards may remain on the table. Revealing a preference for a soft Brexit without removing a hard Brexit from the table is nearly impossible. In the absence of a hard Brexit as a possible outcome a soft Brexit is guaranteed. Then, aligning policy with intentions requires the PM to have as a preference: Soft Brexit $>_{pm}$ Brexit, i.e. better a soft Brexit than any Brexit. This is likely to lead to a clash with Brexit hardliners (BHLs) who prefer to claim Soft Brexit $<_{blh}$ Brexit and who claim (without proof) that Soft Brexit $<_{wop}$ Brexit.

Disappointing initial offer concerning the status of EU citizens. The EU has imposed a structure on the Brexit negotiations, which is supposed to begin with negotiating a divorce settlement, only subsequently to deal with a post Brexit trade agreement. The UK has reluctantly agreed with this schedule, and has simply made an initial offer regarding the status of EU27 citizens within the EU which is remote from EU27/28 preferences. Indeed, for the UK there is nothing to be gained by thinking in terms of (potentially paradoxical) preferences for soft Brexit versus hard Brexit and so on. Getting the divorce settled is a task for the EU as well as for the UK. The EU has agreed to discuss these matters, conclusively, before the soft versus hard question is raised. This can only mean a preliminary assumption of a hard Brexit, including the UK exiting from the jurisdiction of the CJEU.

Casting the issue as pathfinding in a maze. In the long run, the EU27/28 will understand that, finding a workable path for the UK to exit from the EU, is so complex that it will require systematic cooperation from both sides. Moreover, it will sooner or later be understood by the EU27/28 side that effectuating the Brexit decision can only be performed in a credible way (from the UK side) by not getting locked into a network of self-contradictory preferences.

Given the complexity of the puzzle of how to Brexit at all (and given the referendum outcome), it is indeed plausible that working from an initial pro Remain bias is more helpful than having a pro Leave bias as the point of departure, because a pro Leave bias might more easily lead to an underestimation of the problem at hand. By casting the question 'how to Brexit' as a pathfinding problem rather than as solving an optimisation problem it becomes more manageable.

Framing Brexit in terms of immigration control. By framing Brexit in terms of immigration control, and thereby assigning more meaning to the Brexit vote than follows from its mere technical form, the door has been opened for the EU to change itself to become more attractive for the UK, Switzerland, and perhaps other member and non-member states too.

If the president of the EU states that he does not know what kind of Brexit the UK is after, he fails to notice that an obvious opening for precisely this discussion has been put forward by the UK PM, who by doing so risked being considered too single minded by the community of Brexit advocates at large.

Not stretching the will of the people too far. By speaking of Brexit the PM avoids making too much use of 'the will of the people'.[5]

Exiting from the London fisheries convention. The announcement made on 2 July 2017 that the UK intends to withdraw the 1964 London fisheries convention brings home the message to all involved that the UK is not afraid of a hard Brexit.

Inversion of announced preferences. Trivially Brexit is either going to be a no deal hard Brexit, or will be softer than a no deal hard Brexit. Suppose Theresa May prefers to achieve a hard Brexit, based on a good deal. Is there any stronger statement than (i) better no deal than a bad deal, and (ii) better a good deal than no deal, which can be issued at this moment? This seems not to be the case.

---

[5] Remarkably most uses of the phrase 'the will of the people' seem to be made in order to prevent the people from acquiring another chance to express their will. A side-effect of that attitude is that the same binary referendum outcome is used time and again to obtain more and more consequences, which logically speaking cannot be justified. That the UK must leave Euratom, for example,, cannot possibly be inferred from the referendum outcome, neither can the converse.

Consider, for example, the option that UK Brexit negotiators announce a preference for a moderately hard Brexit (see Definition 8.1.2 above) over a no deal hard Brexit. It seems plausible that a higher price must be paid for achieving precisely this outcome, once the EU27/28 side negotiators know of this preference. Suppose the EU negotiators know that the UK prefers a medium Brexit over a moderately hard Brexit. Then it is likely that the EU27/28 negotiators will be less flexible in providing a compromise in terms of opt-outs for freedom of movement of people (into the UK) than if they happened to think that the UK's preferences were the other way around. Thus it makes sense for the UK not to reveal this preference.

If the UK prefers a moderately hard Brexit over a medium Brexit, it may be useful to communicate a preference the other way around and to work towards a very fruitful (for the UK) of the four freedoms that come with a continued ECM membership only to settle for a disappointing (claimed by the UK side) compromise towards a moderately soft Brexit.

By lying about preferences in advance of negotiations, a stronger negotiation position can objectively be achieved. The fact that the electorate has denied Theresa May a significant Commons majority does not imply that she is under an increased pressure to reveal her references during negotiations; in fact, it is rather the other way around.

Asking Labour for support. Although this won't easily be successful by asking all MPs, including oppositional MPs for ideas and support, preparations are made for bipartisan support for the Brexit process.

Not deviating from austerity. By clinging to austerity, thus supporting chancellor Philip Hammond, pressure is mounted on some Brexiters to depart from austerity, thus potentially invoking a split in the group of conservative Brexiters.

Not complaining about the Chancellor's stated preference for a soft Brexit. After the general election the Chancellor has chosen for a position in which a no deal Brexit is portrayed as a mistake to be avoided. This position is close to the Labour position which, though formally advocating a hard Brexit, also frames Brexit in terms of economic objectives and expectations. By being permissive of this position the PM avoids being portrayed as going for a hard Brexit against all cost, while never herself stating anything which excludes a hard Brexit.

The Chancellor's position is somewhat inconsistent (see also Paragraph 8.7 below). He claims that the people have made up their mind, and at the same time he argues for a sensible Brexit, thereby implicating that other interpretations of the referendum outcome may not be sensible. He should of course admit that at most an exit from the EU has emerged as the will of the people and that it is entirely gratuitous to claim that in addition the exit to come must (according to the will of the people) be sensible in a way which the Chancellor is able to determine with any precision.

Dealing with a deaf and blind opponent. Seen from the outside, the EU27/28 position lacks a willingness (or ability) to understand why the EU might be less attractive for the UK than it claims to be, and how the EU might profit from taking such issues seriously. The UK negotiators will have to explain the obvious, and to repeat it many times, and must be prepared to endure the absence of even a bare minimum of understanding.

Negotiation in the absence of reasonable mutual understanding is falsely portrayed as using EU27/28 inhabitants of the UK as bargaining chips. They need not be placed in that role if the EU27/28 side does not insist to both slice and serve the cake. The PM leaves it to other cabinet members to attack EU leaders on these matters.

8.5 On the logic of Brexit II

There are many ways to look at the Brexit phenomenon. Each explanation of parts of the Brexit process can be based on hypotheses. By taking an additional hypothesis on board, not only do the steps taken by the UK government fit in a coherent picture but some remarkable actions by opposition leader Jeremy Corbyn also fit into the same picture.

We shall now adopt, for the sake of the argument, the following hypothesis on Brexit:

> The C&UP has a strong kernel advancing a hard Brexit, the so-called Brexiters. This group has significant, diverse, and stable support within the UK population. No political movement is able to win out against this group given its popular support. The only viable option for opponents of a hard Brexit is to steer towards a state where the Brexiters are confronted with contradictions and obstacles regarding their own positions to such an extent that they will be split as a consequence. Such contradictions may only

arise while actually trying to put Brexit into effect. No form of intellectual or conceptual analysis will suffice, on the contrary, attempts to argue for a soft Brexit on theoretical grounds are likely to be felt as weak (soft in a psychological sense) and are likely to strengthen rather than weaken the Brexiter position.

If Labour intends to replace the Conservative government, then, according to the hypothesis, it must not oppose the Brexiters directly. Not voting on the motion, stating a preference for a soft Brexit, as Jeremy Corbyn has imposed on his MPs, following the 2017 Queen's speech, is the strategy appropriate for not interfering with the process taking place amongst Brexiter rank and file. Labour might not be blamed for obstructing Brexiter policy making, while at the same time, it relentlessly points at the risks involved in a crashed out hard Brexit. Besides, Labour must act as if Brexit constitutes only a minor aspect of today's issues, leaving all propaganda for Brexit to be made by the Brexiters. This activity may become much less rewarding once negative side-effects of the policy towards Brexit become apparent.

8.6 On the Logic of Brexit III

Yet another way to look at Brexit is to perceive it primarily as the success of a single person who managed to influence the public opinion in advance of the referendum. Vote Leave Campaign manager Dominique Cummings has been credited with creating the highly effective slogan 'taking back control' as well as with the equally effective campaign bus advertisement suggesting that £350 M (million) could be rerouted from the EU to the NHS each week.

Both utterances will stand for many years to come as superb landmarks for political campaigning and marketing. It may well be the case that precisely these two slogans have tilted the public towards a majority vote for Leave. Recently Cummings has expressed doubts on the rationale of Brexit and the referendum, claims in a tweet that having the referendum was not a good idea, and that the UK should instead have sought other ways to promote its interests within the EU first.

Putting forward the slogan 'taking back control' can hardly be criticised. Whether or not the UK fares well when being equipped with more control is another matter and is left to the voter's judgement.

The £350 M for NHS suggestion has frequently been referred to as a lie. Indeed the quantification of the UK's monthly contribution to the EU budget should rather have been £250 M. So here is a 'lie'. Mentioning the NHS as an alternative destination of that money cannot constitute a lie. Returning to the falsity of the numerical figure the following though experiment may be of use: (i) if the referendum had been lost, i.e. remaining in the EU would be winning, nobody would ever look back at this figure and merely forget it as one of many imprecise utterances that are bound to occur in any serious political battle, (ii) after a landslide victory for Leave the figure would be forgotten as having had only marginal impact on voting behavior, (iii) after a marginal win for Leave (the actual outcome) the guess might be coined that the figure £350 M (rather than £250 M which is considered to have been the correct figure) was crucial, (iv) but then it would be hard to believe that the media effect of posting £250 M on the campaign bus would have been much less effective, even if it is admitted that the text on the bus has been the decisive marketing factor.

Now one may ask: has it been morally wrong (say for Cummings) to show an incorrect figure on the bus. At this stage in the argument it is relevant that Cummings made no secret of the advisory status of the referendum, a fact which in his view was supportive for voting Leave. Now suppose, in hindsight the MPs are looking for ways not to comply with the referendum outcome after all. It may then be used as a fact that in the final stage of the campaign Vote Leave announced a lie so that the people have undeniably been misled. By posting a manifest and unnecessary lie on the bus Cummings has offered the MPs a plot for a potential way out of an unwanted Brexit if that is needed, an action which is morally justifiable rather than irresponsible or morally wrong.

8.7 News, facts, and 'alternative facts'

Most communications concerning Brexit take the form of news, the news being that someone says something. What is said is often presented as a fact, and opponents of the speaker may often label said fact as an 'alternative fact', i.e. a fact which the speaker themselves know to be false.[6]

We will consider one such news item in more detail. Chancellor Philip Hammond has repeatedly said (June 2017) that the people did not vote to get poorer. True, they voted to Leave the EU. But making an inference from this outcome to

---

[6] We will adopt the language that facts may be true or false, with 'alternative facts', those facts anyone knows to be false. Such false facts need not be labelled as lies in case the intention of announcing the fact was not to convince an audience of its truth but rather to communicate some other state of affairs or opinion.

an economic intention is unfounded. Hammond's interpretation of the referendum outcome is quite dubious. Had the referendum outcome been pro Remain they would not have voted to be poorer either. Hammond favoured Remain in advance of the referendum, and taking the economic perspective for so important as he does now and most plausibly did then, he is likely to have thought in advance of the referendum that the economic odds were in favour of Remain rather than of Leave.

In Hammond's view, the people may well have voted to become poorer, but that they accepted this price in the light of other advantages. Hammond's representation of the election outcome may be considered a deceit or 'alternative fact', as a more plausible reading of the election outcome was that the people were not impressed by the risk of some economic hardship ahead. Warnings that Brexit would initially create an economic downturn had been issued all over the place, including most official sources.

Shifting the framing of Brexit from immigration to prosperity without demonstrating how, in Hammond's view, Brexit can outperform non-Brexit in economic terms is unconvincing. Philip Hammond's interpretation of the referendum outcome is paradoxical whereas the interpretation (framing in terms of immigration) of Theresa May is not. Predicting the consequences of this grandiose difference is not so easy but sooner or later a choice must be made.

8.8 Redesigning the Brexit process in hindsight

The Brexit process shows clear signs of having been ill-defined from the start, as it leads to so many unpredicted events, and to so many questions which ought to have been taken into account in a public manner in advance of the referendum.[7] The almost predictable rise of 'cheap' political swipes, stoney faced brinkmanship, and finger-pointing by all sides has brought only uncertainty and, arguably, even less trust in the political classes than at the outset. A way to redesign the process might have been as follows:

1. Move in a cheap and efficient manner towards a medium Brexit with the UK in a somewhat adapted single market ESM, and within the customs union ECU. Moreover, plan a second referendum about leaving the (modified) ESM four years after the UK has left the EU.

---

[7] These flaws have been outlined in detail in Nikolka & Poutvaara 2016 [16].

2. If the second referendum yielded a majority for staying within the ESM, have negotiations on how to improve that setting for both the UK and EU27 (or its successor entity if it has changed). If a majority votes for leaving the ESM was obtained, then work towards a moderately hard Brexit, and again plan a referendum for 4 years later in which the question is whether or not to exit from ECU and ECJ (and related issues).

3. If the 3th referendum indicated that the people preferred to stay in the ECU, finalise the arrangement by negotiating once more, in order to find an optimal structure for both the UK and the EU27. Otherwise, effectuating a hard Brexit is without any doubt The Will Of The People, and that must be negotiated and put into practice.

This process takes a period of 14 years at most, which seems long, but might be compared to the 43 years that it has taken to arrive at the current status quo. This way of working would have allowed all sides to minimise the risk of irreversible and pointless damage to the UK or to EU27.

9

Concluding remarks

In this work, we have begun to apply promise theory to the vastly complicated network of events, intentions, and statements that have been made about Brexit. There are two reasons to do this: the first is that we believe that promises offer a lens through which one sees clearly the distinctions between rational alternative and the impossibility of rational choice, helping to assess the logical consistency of statements amongst other things. Few other frameworks (e.g. dialects of logic) could hope to cope with the muddle of actors, states, and categories in what is happening before our eyes. Thus, as a means of impartial appraisal, we have found that it brings a particular clarity to the topic. At the same time, the discussion serves as a case study on promise theory, with a strong human element. Examples of this kind that are rarely available in public view. Considering Brexit in terms of promises thus appears to provide uniform perspective. Here are some conclusions. Two types of conclusions are drawn, conclusions about Brexit and conclusions about promise theory.

9.1 Conclusions concerning Brexit

Taking promises as a uniform approach, the following conclusions became apparent:

1. The arguments in favour of Brexit range from academic and abstract to emotion-driven one-liners: the latter frequently being wrapped promise-like assertions.

2. There are no grounds for inferring, from the outcome of the June 2016

Referendum, that a majority of voters has accepted or adopted a specific bundle of promises about Brexit that were made in advance of the referendum by leading Brexiters.

3. The promises made in favour of Brexit may have been noisy and inconsistent, even deceitful, but this makes little difference for to the outcome. Even if each of these referendum promises were dropped, a comprehensible and potentially convincing argument for the UK to leave the EU remains in place.

4. The idea that those who voted for Brexit, thereby accepted the four pro Leave promises as listed above in Paragraph 1.5.1 is not convincing. Arguments for a Brexit which deviate from these specific promises can be easily found.

5. The combination of promises made in the 2015 Conservative Manifesto and in the subsequent Queen's Speech which contains an announcement of the referendum as well, does not imply a binding status for the referendum. These promises are consistent with the referendum having had an advisory status.

6. Assigning a binding status to the referendum outcome, as it emerged, is very similar to making a promise create a binding obligation. The logical complexity of the obligation creates more confusion than one may have expected at first. There is an asymmetry here: if the outcome had been remain nobody it would have been logically unproblematic to assign that outcome a binding status, while with an outcome for leave, the fact that leaving can be performed in so many different ways creates a conceptual problem. Precisely such problems promise theory intends to avoid when proposing promises as a tool for systems design.

7. The so-called hard Brexit is not a clearly defined outcome on which the UK can always fall back. The UK will have to negotiate its way into an effective WTO membership with many external parties some of who may not even be sympathetic with the idea of the UK becoming a new WTO member. Several issues will require a negotiated agreement in the WTO Brexit approach as well. ECHC membership, arrangements around Euratom and ESA, agricultural subsidies, participation in selected EU activities in science and research. The situation is made more complex,

rather than simpler, for the UK if crashing out rather than exiting on the basis of an exit agreement with EU27/28 is taking place.

8. Article 50 of the Lisbon Treaty does not prepare an exit in such a manner that an orderly exit can be convincingly managed. Theresa May has now been cornered into the position that (i) Brexit will be a success, but (ii) this success is so hard to deliver that only she can do it herself. A remarkable position by all means.

    The lack of clarity about the trade agreements to be expected after a state has left the EU is a roadblock that stands in the way of a sound process. Promise theoretically, some form of baseline ought to have been agreed, not in procedural terms, but in terms of its *desired outcome* target.

    It would, for example, have been quite reasonable had the UK first worked from within the EU towards a much more detailed phrasing of Article 50. In other words: Article 50 falls short of being helpful when it comes to putting Brexit into effect. This problem constitutes a joint responsibility for the UK and EU27/28. Neither side seems able or willing to convince the public that it must live up to that responsibility.

    Performing a renegotiation of the Lisbon Treaty, in order to prepare for a more predictable exit process for any EU member in advance of Brexit negotiations, might be an option.

9. Non-compliance of the EU27 with the Eurozone treaty may be construed as a financially quantifiable claim from the UK on EU27/28. This claim may well be as large, or even much larger, as any exit fee that EU27/28 wishes to impose on the UK as a condition on subsequent negotiations on the form that Brexit will take (WTO-Brexit, EEA Brexit, EFTA Brexit, ECHR Brexit, etc.)

    The track record of EU27/28 states on compliance with its own promised agreements is not good. Here lies a plausible risk for the all EU27/28 sides: following a split, the EU27 may not even be able to abide by its promises as agreed in the settlement.

10. The complaints, sometimes heard from EU27/28 politicians, that the UK intends to perform so-called cherry picking, (and that this is not a good thing) is baseless in the light of the fact that there is no guarantee that the UK can exit the EU without the need of special arrangements. Comparing the UK (65 million people across four diverse regions) to Norway (5

million people) or Liechtenstein (37 thousand people) is likely to involve a gross oversimplification, and the idea that a similar deal can be easily manufactured may be implausible.

11. The fact that almost every EU citizen is taught English, with the effect that living in the UK is an option for relatively many EU27 citizens, creates an asymmetry which has been insufficiently taken into account when adoption of the free flow of people is required from all EU members in a symmetric manner.

12. None of the procedural difficulties with implementing Brexit constitute solid reasons for the UK to remain in the EU. On the contrary, many of these complications point to weaknesses in the EU system.

13. The phrase 'taking back control' may be used used about the opportunities that Brexit presents to EU27/28. Taking back control (in the UK) over the financial industry, the car industry, and Academia, and on the long run also in terms of military prominence. Taking back control by EU27/28 is best served by adopting a pro WTO Brexit bias, even if that induces a lot of collateral damage to EU27/28 trade.

14. EU27/28 is in need of reforms that provide more room for policy diversity between member states, otherwise the risk is too high that Brexit won't be the last event of its kind.

9.2 Conclusions regarding promise theory

This book takes events into account up to the second week of July 2017. This date is arbitrary, but we need to choose some endpoint for writing the case study on promise theory that is our primary aim.

As an application of promise theory, we have found much clarity results from the use of the basic axioms: agents may not make promises on behalf of others than themselves, without loss of certainty. Moreover, the promises made have often not been accepted, and cannot be assessed, making them frequently spurious.

1. The fundamental thesis underlying Bergstra & Burgess [1] and prior work by Mark Burgess is that promises become maximally useful as a control mechanism once it is assumed that obligations (be it moral or legal) are

not created as a side-effect of promising. Instead an update of expectations by promisee and other agents in scope is the primary effect of promising and a continuous (or repeated) update of trust in the promiser (during the life-cycle of the promise) is the primary side-effect of issuing a promise.

Brexit provides a remarkable application of precisely this idea as illustrated in 2.6 above. If promises had been understood as not producing obligations the conceptual difficulties of understanding the referendum outcome would have been solved, and the political consequences of a formalistic reading of the referendum outcome would have been avoided.

2. Labelling an assertion as a promise can be done without being worried about truth or validity of the statement. This is a striking advantage of thinking in terms of promises. In the case of Brexit it is the rule rather than the exception that promises do not create obligations, which validates the contention taken in the promise theory, as set out in [1].

3. While promises occur frequently in the context of Brexit, the withdrawal of promises is far less common in this case. Promises that were made in the C&UP manifesto for the June 2017 general election and which have not been repeated in the subsequent Queen's Speech (such as the promise to reconsider permission of fox hunting so that it may become legal again) may be considered as having been put forward as candidates for being withdrawn. Formal withdrawal, or significant delay, may take place after the Queen's Speech has been approved.

   Promises concerning the unfolding of Brexit which have been reconfirmed in the Queen's Speech in its approved form, have obtained the support required for an appeal to the Salisbury Doctrine when it comes to a debate with the Lords. For other promises in the conservative manifesto obtaining such support still requires forthcoming support by a majority of MPs.

4. Assessment of promises takes place in different phases, which lends much flexibility to the notion of a promise. This flexibility is relevant in the case of Brexit. In particular plausibility functions as a pre-assessment in advance of any a judgement about the promise having been kept. The dynamics of trust in a promiser is discussed in Chapter 10 of [1].

5. Changes of context, i.e. state transitions, such as new results of elections

and votes, as well as crucial policy decisions, made by parties involved can be taken into account as transformers of promises, mainly by either adapting the conditions for a promise when one or more of these are becoming true or by having a promise expired as soon as at least one of its conditions turn out to be invalid.

6. The number of promises playing a role in the Brexit process around the time of the referendum is remarkably high. Indeed it seems to be impossible to provide a convincing description of the process without taking promises into account. The net effect of too many promises (as a network phenomenon) could end up in self-cancelling purpose.

7. Very few promises are actually accepted by any agent or interested party (promise type −), and even fewer promises are kept. Promises have arguably been used as rallying cries rather than expected outcomes. Most promises remain pending until Brexit is actually effectuated, and are unlikely to be keepable, as they violate the autonomy principle.

8. Promises which are contained in a party manifesto of a party that may obtain a majority in a general election serve a particular purpose of being hooks for the argument that the Lords must, on the matter of that promise, collectively and ultimately, follow a government resulting from said majority (if it comes true). A promise included in the manifesto may be understood as a warning for the electorate: a proposal for the implementation of one or more of such promises will (or at least may) not be turned down by a House of Lords known disagree even with a large majority with the promised plans. Reconfirmation of the promise in the subsequent Queen's Speech may be understood as an indication that a forthcoming appeal to the application of the Salisbury Doctrine is not ruled out. Such promises play four roles at the same time:

    (a) Informing the public about an intention (the primary role of a promise), thereby:

    (b) Updating their conditional expectation concerning the expectation of effectuation of the plan, conditional on the election outcome;

    (c) Warning the public of a potential application of the Salisbury Doctrine (an additional factor which increases the expectation just mentioned)[1], and:

---

[1] The hung Parliament that resulted after the general election of June 2017 gives rise to the

(d) Limiting the freedom of impactful judgement of the House of Lords.

This nexus of roles illustrates the remarkable complexity of the concept of promises. One may prefer to do away with promises altogether and to analyse Brexit and similar phenomena in terms of simpler conceptual categories (e.g. rhetoric by authority). It is unlikely that there is a simpler formal approach, however, because of the atomic nature of promises, which defeats analysing a promise as a conjunction of more basic actions or communications.

We have no opinion on that matter, as we merely examine what can be achieved by taking promises as a point of departure, whatever unavoidable complexity it might entail. Our conclusion is that looking at Brexit in terms of promises is informative in spite of any limitations of the approach.

9. Thinking of promises in terms of underlying biases, as well as in terms of the evolution of such biases, provides a useful insight in the dynamics of the portfolio of promises though a progression of state transitions.

10. Although trust in a promiser may induce a promisee to assess a promise as plausible, the complementary mechanism (that a promisee trusts those promisers who promise an action or state of affairs which is close to what they already think, i.e. confirmation bias) seems to be more relevant to what we have seen. Promising what a promiser wants to hear may create trust, even if the promise itself is a deception or an outright lie.[2]

9.3 Non-occurrence of Brexit, can it happen?

Can the process leading to Brexit be stopped or reversed? Except for very clear remarks recently made by Vince Cable (in his capacity of being the prospective leader of the Liberal MPs) about the huge complexity of Brexit and the need to

---

non-trivial question to what extent promises included in the opposition manifesto may be brought forward in the case made for an application to the Salisbury Doctrine even if the opposition (post election) would disagree with doing so. Such constitutional matter lie outside the scope of this paper but the resolution of this question will have an impact on the semantics of promises made in future manifestos.

[2] Following the first definition of a lie in Mahon 2016 [14] a promise with qualifier [+] can indeed qualify as a lie.

contemplate the mere possibility that Brexit cannot be put into effect because of said complexity, this question hardly receives any attention at the time of writing (July 2017), but it is a relevant question nevertheless. The advisory status of the referendum still stands and the MPs may at any time change their view on the matter, with a potential change of a majority view as a consequence. The MPs may conclude that novel facts have arisen (provided that is the case) which stand in the way of putting into effect the will of the people concerning Brexit as it had been extracted from the referendum by the Commons and confirmed by the Lords when discussing the triggering of Article 50. New facts may come about in different ways, here are some options for such events:

1. The case has been made that the referendum was flawed by not taking votes of potential voters outside the UK properly into account. The legal ramifications of this argument have not yet been sorted out fully. Conceivably this approach may shed a new light on the validity of the referendum outcome.

2. It has been argued that the appeal to Article 50 was flawed because there had not been a preceding Parliamentary decision to leave the EU. This observation may eventually have some impact, but it is hard to see how it can lead to a change of direction as all members of Parliament seem to have understood the the decision taking process leading up to triggering Article 50 as having been adequate from a procedural viewpoint.

3. The legal issue which may arise from noticing that leaving the EU and leaving the EEA is not the same step, and possibly cannot be effectuated in one go, may cause delay and may have currently unpredictable side-effects. EEA membership has its own exit rules according to some, even if the EEA membership is of the kind that just comes with EU membership.

4. Technical problems such as the need for continued EURATOM membership under an CJEU umbrella may impose constraints that are hard to satisfy.

5. Complaints about the so-called lies during the referendum campaign may in hindsight successfully discredit key Brexiters thereby causing a public rethink of the entire matter.

   It is rather difficult to imagine that a legal case can be made out of these lies for the following reasons (i) both sides of the argument have been at fault in some cases (ii) whether or not some utterance qualifies as a lie is hardly decidable, (iii) probabilistic predictions cannot be lies, and (iv) increasingly importantly, because during the referendum campaign not much was known about how Brexit would be implemented upon a vote for Leave.

If the UK, upon accepting the vote for Leave, had made a principled and parliamentary decision to work towards Brexit and then had taken 3 to 5 years in order to prepare for triggering article 50, including the option to ask for a preparatory renegotiation of article 50, probably nobody would now (one year after the referendum) be bothered much about either the validity of various arguments that played a role during the campaign or the explanatory value of specific and possibly dubious arguments for the outcome of the referendum.

6. The occurrence or announcement of significant internal reforms within the EU which solve one or more of the UK's most pressing worries.

7. New and significant worries about the economic future of the UK outside the EU, in combination with a sustained framing of the referendum outcome in economic terms rather than in terms of immigration control.

8. New general elections in the UK (that is after the June 2017 election) may become necessary when the current government (C&UP with support from DUP) runs into an unresolvable problem, potentially remote from Brexit.

A second 'premature' general election may bring quite different forces into power. A new government may turn out to be committed to uncover the degree to which the referendum has been influenced by commercial media power. The need to have a far more impartial Brexit referendum may be felt much stronger than at this moment, and a government may decide to hold a second referendum on the matter.

9. The very objective of reducing immigration may become discredited, first of all by finally recognising the home made (and EU independent) character of today's UK immigration count (and disavow Brexit proponents who preferred to replace such facts by 'alternative facts' (deceptions) which suited them better). Secondly, it could be discredited by becoming aware that the challenge for the UK lies in recruiting new workers from EU27 states, rather than by producing contra-globalisation obstacles that may

discourage them from coming to the UK.[3]

10. Theoretical analysis of the referendum as a social choice mechanism in this particular case may bring about the idea that a second referendum about EU membership is justified, and a second referendum may lead to a different result.

11. The very idea that the will of the people concerning a complex topic may be reduced (encoded in) to a single bit of information may be challenged, and a second extraction of the will of the people may create inconsistent results.

12. The proposition that no deal is better than a bad deal may be challenged if no deal is achieved and if no deal is considered too problematic an outcome.

13. At some stage the UK Government may prefer to withdraw (revoke, withdraw from) the Article 50 process and to plan its activation again in a later stage once many more issues have been sorted out by way of preparation.[4]

    The first year after the referendum has served as an educational phase in which many UK citizens (and politicians) have become aware of (i) strengths and weaknesses of the EU, (ii) the complexity of the EU, (iii) the many legal constructions that have been accumulated in connection with the EU, the large menu of options for post Brexit relations with the EU27, (iv) the role of foreigners in the UK economy, and (v) the sheer complexity of achieving an orderly Brexit. Restarting the exit process after some time might enable the UK to be better prepared for it.

None of these scenarios are particularly likely to occur, but none can be ruled out either, not even on the time scale of the Brexit negotiations.

---

[3] Upon becoming leading MP of the Liberals Vince Cable has started an offensive claiming that Theresa May as a home secretary failed to realise the immigration targets she had defined herself, targets which are impractical and unjustified according to Cable. Moreover he claims that May successfully turned this failure into the misinformed public conviction that immigration had grown out of control, thereby willingly supporting the case for Brexit.

[4] It is a matter of legal debate whether or not the UK Government can unilaterally halt the exit process as specified by Article 50 and return to the state before it was triggered. It is hardly conceivable that referendum voters could have had an informed opinion on this matter at the time of the referendum.

9.4 A comment on promises in relation to policy

We are not aware of any logic that can uniquely integrate promises and preferences into a stable prediction of outcomes, based on the result of a referendum. Even provided with a detailed litany of promises, by all parties, one is unable to infer a clear picture of such a broad body of interests. Cast in the light of promises, the UK referendum on Brexit is left with the taint of a miscalculated piece of political theatre, whose main result has been to temporarily polarise UK and EU citizens into adversarial positions, and thus provide the impetus to take the step into the unknown. There is no way of predicting what the outcome of the following process might look like, because in a complex network, the path one takes does matter. Populist promises have thus reduced complex issues to simplistic terms, which will ultimately leave voters unsatisfied when outcomes do materialise.

What strikes us, after this investigation, is the extent to which the keystone promise underpinning all democracy (that a government fairly represents its people through voting) fails to plausibly capture the sentiments of a network of culturally disparate parties, where information has rendered national borders less relevant than at any earlier time in history. Perhaps it is politics itself that is outdated in the information age. The oversimplification of positions, at times, inflames tensions, especially in the case of global versus local issues: examples of this are springing up all across the globe. It certainly poses interesting questions for the future of collective bargaining in political processes, in a world where rich information tends to diversify rather than unify opinion.

References

[1] Jan Bergstra and Mark Burgess. *Promise Theory: Principles and Applications.* χt Axis Press. ISBN9781495437779 (2014).

[2] Alexander Beunder. Brexit deel 2: de rationele economische motieven van laagopgeleiden & ouderen. `https://economielinks.wordpress.com/2016/07/05/brexit-deel-2-de-rationele-economische-motieven -van-lager-opgeleiden-ouderen/` (accessed May 20, 2017), (2014).

[3] Mark Burgess. *Thinking in Promises: Designing Systems for Cooperation.* O'Reilly Media (2015).

[4] Francesco Capriglione. Brexit: an anti-historical divorce which can change the EU. `https://papers.ssrn.com/sol3/papers.cfm?abstract_id=2839395`, (2016).

[5] Swati Dhingra and Thomas Samspon. Life after Brexit: what are the UK's options outside the European union? `http://eprints.lse.ac.uk/66143/` (2016).

[6] Helena Djurkovic and Anand Menon. Brexit and beyond, how the United Kingdom might leave the European Union. `http://ukandeu.ac.uk/wp-content/uploads/2016/11/Brexit-and-Beyond-how-the-UK-might-leave-the-EU.pdf` (accessed May 25, 2017), (2016).

[7] Glenn Dymond and Hugo Deadman. The Salisbury Doctrine. *The House of Lords Library, Library Note 2006/006,*`http://www.parliament.uk/documents/lords-library/hllsalisburydoctrine.pdf`, (2006)

[8] Piet Eeckhout and Eleni Frantziou. Brexit and Article 50 TEU: a constitutional reading. Working paper, UCL European institute, `https://www.ucl.ac.uk/european-institute/brexit-article-50.pdf` (accessed May 30, 2017), (2016).

[9] Gerda Falkner. Is the EU a Non-Compliance Community? Towards 'compliance for credibility' and EU action for the protection of democracy in Europe. *Les Cahiers Europeens de Sciences Po. No. 01/2013.* `https://www.sciencespo.fr/centre-etudes-europeennes/sites/sciencespo.fr.centre-etudes-europeennes/files/n_1_2013_Falkner_final.pdf` (accessed May 15, 2017), (2013).

[10] Ioannis Glinavos. Brexit law suits–but not as you know them. Verfassungsblog /on constitutional matters `http://verfassungsblog.de/brexit-lawsuits-but-not-as-you-know-them/` (accessed July 6, 2017), (2017).

[11] Erik Kaufman. It's NOT the economy, stupid: Brexit as a story of personal values. `http://blogs.lse.ac.uk/politicsandpolicy/personal-values-brexit-vote/` (accessed May 20, 2017), (2017).

[12] Bruno Latour. . *Reassembling the social: An introduction to actor-network-theory.* Oxford university press, (2005).

[13] Adrian Low. Brexit is not the will of the British people–it never has been. `http://blogs.lse.ac.uk/brexit/2016/10/24/brexit-is-not-the-will-of-the-british-people-it-never-has-been/` (accessed June 22, 2017), (2016).

[14] James Edwin Mahon. The definition of lying and deception. The Stanford Encyclopedia of Philosophy (Winter 2016 Edition), Edward N. Zalta (ed.), `https://plato.stanford.edu/archives/win2016/entries/lying-definition/` (2016).

[15] Patrick Minford, Sakshi Gupta. Vo Phuong Mai Le, Vidya Mahambare and Yongdeng Xu. *Should Britain Leave the EU?: an economic analysis of a troubled relationship.* Edward Elgar Publishing (2015).

[16] Till Nikolka and Panu Poutvaara. Brexit–theory and empirics. CESifo Forum 4, (2016).

[17] Tim Oliver. Europe without Britain–assessing the impact on then European Union of a British withdrawal. *SWP Research Paper, Berlin,*

`http://ketlib.lib.unipi.gr/xmlui/bitstream/handle/ket/491/Europe%20without%20Britain.pdf?sequence=1`(accessed May 24, 2017), (2013).

[18] Tim Oliver. The EU's unwillingness to discuss the possibility of a 'Brexit' is playing into the hands of Eurosceptics. LSE European Institute `http://bit.ly/16c6z95` (accessed May 22, 2017), (2013).

[19] Tim Oliver. Theory and Brexit: can theoretical approaches help us to understand Brexit? LSE European Institute, `http://blogs.lse.ac.uk/brexit/2017/03/14/theory-and-brexit-can-theoretical-approaches-help-us-understand-brexit/` (accessed July 5, 2017), (2017).

[20] Jean Pisani-Ferry, Norbert Röttgen, André Sapir, Paul Tucker and Guntram B. Wolff. Europe after Brexit: A proposal for a continental partnership. Bruegel External Publication, Brussls (2016).

[21] Julia Rampen. Parliament will trigger Article 50–but may legally still be possible to cancel Brexit. New Statesman, `http://www.newstatesman.com/politics/staggers/2017/02/parliament-will-trigger-article-50-it-may-legally-still-be-possible-cancel` (accessed May 30, 2017), (2017).

[22] Danhong Zhang. Maastricht Treaty–not yet set in stone. *DW made for minds*, `http://www.dw.com/en/maastricht-treaty-not-yet-set-in-stone/a-37435390` (accessed May 15, 2017), (2017).

About the authors

Jan Bergstra is a Dutch computer scientist, living in Utrecht. He has worked at the Institute of Applied Mathematics and Computer Science of the University of Leiden, and the Centrum Wiskunde & Informatica (CWI) in Amsterdam. In 1985 he became Professor of Programming and Software Engineering at the Informatics Institute of the University of Amsterdam and Professor of Applied Logic at Utrecht University. He has retired in December 2016, and now works as an independent researcher and consultant. His work has focussed on logic and the theoretical foundations of software engineering, with an emphasis on algebraic methods for the specification of data and of computational processes in general.

Mark Burgess is a British theoretical physicist, turned computer scientist, living in Oslo, Norway. After authoring and consulting for the IT industry and holding a number of research and teaching positions, he was appointed Professor of Network and System Administration at Oslo University College in 2005, which he held until resigning in 2011 to found the CFEngine company. He is the originator of the globally used CFEngine software as well as founder of CFEngine AS, Inc. He is the author of many books and scientific publications, and is a frequent speaker at international events.

Mark Burgess may be found at `www.markburgess.org`, and on Twitter under the name `@markburgess_osl`.